ABOUT THE AUTHOR

Mike Lipkin is president of Environics/Lipkin, a global research and motivation company based in Toronto. He is also an international strategic coach, facilitator and catalyst for high performance.

Mike combines his learning from talking to a million people in 43 countries with Environics Social Values research to offer clients the best of all worlds: a powerful blend of ideas and principles that help them achieve remarkable results.

Mike was raised in South Africa and immigrated to Canada in 2001. He is renowned for his ability to blend humour with content that inspires people into action. This is his seventh book.

D0111006

PRAISE FOR MIKE LIPKIN

"Everyone loved your presentation and found it highly relevant and powerfully motivating."
STEPHEN GRAHAM, Chief Operating Officer, Questrade

"You did a wonderful job engaging our team and provided an excellent message, well done! Thank you for sharing your expertise as a storyteller, and providing insights in a very compelling and charismatic manner."
STEVE WALLMER, Chief Sales Officer, Vice President, HUB International Barton

"Mike, you were awesome. The feedback has been universally and enthusiastically positive."
BETTY DELBIANCO, Chief Legal and Administrative Officer, Celestica

"We received very positive feedback on the program from the members, with an overall rating of 4.9 out of 5. Thanks again for contributing to such a great agenda."
RICHARD BRISBOIS, Senior Research Associate & Executive Network Manager, Leadership and Human Resources Research, The Conference Board of Canada

"Your messages were extremely well received, timely to what we are going through, and presented in a way that really helped everyone engage. Making people uncomfortable in a fun way is actually a great way to drive self-awareness. I've taken away several of your quotes and now have them up on my whiteboard!! Your candor and willingness to push our thinking was terrific."
TAMMI LISSON, Senior Vice President Operations, Canadian Banking, RBC Royal Bank

"Mike, a heartfelt thanks for your performance. I have received countless emails from colleagues commenting on the impact it made to their day. This is just the outcome we were looking for!"
CLAIRE CLINDINNING, Human Performance Consultant, BMO Financial Group

"Mike, we continue to receive amazing feedback on your presentation at the Roadshows. Employees really get the 'investment' that we made bringing you in to motivate and inspire... Awesome! Thank you again for all you did to make these the best roadshows ever for the North American Phone Channel."
VALERIE MINES, Senior Manager, Employee Experience and Engagement, NA Phone Channel Shared Services, TD Bank Group

"Thank you for a fantastic session. Your delivery was amazing and I continue to receive extremely positive feedback. Everyone was thrilled at how you were able to keep the group engaged and energized throughout the entire session. Your authenticity and ability to go with the flow, challenge appropriately, and deal with unpredictability were extremely impressive."
FAITH TULL, Chief People Officer, Randstad Canada

"I can't thank you enough for your WOW keynote presentation. I have had multiple delegates comment to me on what an excellent presentation it was. The whole message really resonated with me personally."
JENNIFER ENGELE, Brand Communications Manager, Pharmasave Drugs (National) Ltd.

"We enjoyed the two days with you and we learnt very important advice, tools, and messages that we will use in our business and personal lives. Mike, the quality of information and knowledge you have shared with us is equal to 100 years of experience."
HATEM KAWASMY, Managing Partner, KPMG Amman Office

"Mike rated amongst the highest of all inspirational speakers and guests we have invited to our Annual Team Meeting. Boomers to Millennials were immediately drawn to Mike's message and powerful delivery."
JIM CASE, CEO, Travelers Financial Group

"Thank you for the terrific presentation and content at our National Sales Meeting. The way you involved our people was phenomenal. I am receiving outstanding feedback."
DAVE O'NEIL, General Manager, Zimmer Biomet Canada

"A HUGE THANK YOU for the incredible performance at the Dell Canada Partner Summit. Your commitment, service, and support were key to our success."
MICHEL LAGACÉ, Senior Manager, Dell Canada Marketing

"You did a great job of corralling and engaging the group with some very good/focused content. It has been a pleasure working with you."
JACQUELINE FOLEY, Chief Marketing Officer, Odgers Berndtson

The 7 secrets to thriving
on massive change so
the best people want to
partner with you

DANCING
WITH
DISRUPTION

MIKE LIPKIN

ENVIRONICS/LIPKIN
RESEARCHED MOTIVATION & PERSUASION

Environics/Lipkin Inc.
33 Bloor Street East, Suite 1020
Toronto, Ontario
Canada M4W 3H1
www.mikelipkin.com

Cataloguing data available from Library and Archives Canada

ISBN 978-1-7751225-0-0 (paperback)
ISBN 978-1-7751225-2-4 (ebook)
ISBN 978-1-7751225-1-7 (audiobook)

Produced by Page Two
www.pagetwostrategies.com

Cover and interior design by Peter Cocking

Printed and bound in Canada by Marquis

**Hunt breakthroughs.
Expect miracles.**

CONTENTS

OMG

Tensions are high and running higher.

Resources are tight and getting tighter.

It's an open-and-shut case. Either you're open
to extreme change or you'll be shut down by it.

'M SURPRISED. I'M amazed. I'm shocked. I'm devastated. I'm horrified. I'm flabbergasted. I'm blown away. I'm astonished. I'm overwhelmed. I'm ecstatic. I'm gutted. WOW! And that's just this morning. It's the exact opposite of *Groundhog Day*. And Forrest Gump only got it half right: life is like a box of chocolates—you never know when they're going to explode.

Every morning, I wake up in a fright because I don't know what happened during the night. But I do know that something happened during the night that will impact me. I know that something in the world will occur today that is going to change my world. It never seems as though I'm ready for it but I always seem to get through it. I expect the unexpected but I'm always surprised.

Sometimes I get surprises I love. Those are the surprises that I'm trying to seed every day. They thrill me. They make me believe in miracles all over again. And sometimes I get the surprises I hate. The moment I discover them, I feel nauseated, weakened, panic-stricken and puny. They make me doubt myself right down to my DNA.

Sound familiar so far? We're all unique, just like everybody else. The exact surprises may change but surprise itself is the new normal. It's called disruption.

Disruption can be a *force majeure*—an act of God that literally changes the landscape or blows things away. Or it can be an act of man or woman that shatters the status quo and redefines our marketplace. The sources of disruption may be disparate but their impact is the same: we're forced to question everything we believe and begin again. Something expires and something originates in the same moment.

Ambivalence is not an option. Doubt is not allowed. Apathy is obsolete. Fatigue must be overcome. Whatever else you decide, you must choose a way. You must choose a mindset. You must choose a philosophy. You must choose a course. You must be cause in the matter. You must *be* the disruptor.

If you think I'm being extreme, I'm already succeeding. I'm confronting you with the first dilemma of disruption: you have to be comfortable being uncomfortable. You have to be willing to go first. Sometimes you might even have to go too far in order to go far enough. The alternative is to be the disruptee. It means playing the victim while you search for blame, not breakthroughs. It means feeling miserable while you feel helpless. It means following others' dreams while you live a nightmare. Things don't have to be awful for them to be a nightmare. They just have to be ho-hum. Middle of the road is where you get run over. Average is purgatory.

One thing is for certain. No matter how chaotic things are right now, they're the calmest they're ever going to be. No matter how fast things are moving, they're moving at the slowest pace they're ever going to move. It only gets more interesting from here. As the ancient Chinese curse states, "May you live in interesting times."

Ambivalence is
not an option.

In my book, however, living in interesting times is a blessing. It's an invitation to be extraordinary. It's the future. This is not a time to pull back. It's not a time to understate your potential or inhibit your influence. This time requires a passion for the grind that sharpens you up, not wears you down. The people around you are hungry for your contribution. They want to be inspired to excel and they want to be exhilarated. They may not even know exactly what they want, but they'll know it when they see it. As the founder of Red Bull, Dietrich Mateschitz, said, "If we don't create the market, it doesn't exist." Mateschitz clearly understood that if you don't demonstrate your value, you won't be valuable. It's as simple as that.

"The breakthrough innovations come when the tension is greatest and the resources are most limited," says leading strategist, Clayton Christensen. "That's when people are actually a lot more open to rethinking the fundamental way they do business."

Tensions are high and running higher. Resources are tight and getting tighter. It's an open-and-shut case. Either you're open to extreme change or you'll be shut down by it. Where do you stand? Are you willing to change the world around you? Are you willing to take a leap even though you could fall? I'm counting on you to take the leap and so are many others. If you go first, somebody, somewhere, will be inspired into action that will inspire someone else somewhere and the virtuous cycle will continue.

Rethinking the fundamental way in which you do business means rethinking the fundamental way in which you think and act. It means consciously re-evaluating your relationship with your environment and your community so you can reset and re-engage for success. The alternative is oblivion. Nothing is more obsolete than someone who is a prisoner of the past.

Do you feel ready to move on? Can you handle the truths? Are you up for the adventure?

Then let's dance.

How to use this book

The phrase I most like to hear from others is, "I never thought of it that way." Sometimes a mere nuance can make a massive difference. Often all it takes is a slight pivot in your direction to discover a whole new vista of opportunity.

That's how I want you to read this book. Don't agree immediately with what I say. Just don't immediately disagree with it. Be open to thinking differently. Resist the temptation to state, "that's wrong" or "that could never work" or "that's impossible." You can decide what to take away and what to leave behind at the end of the book. Until then, ask yourself a simple question: "How can this insight help me to give others what they need?"

Every breakthrough has a gestation period. Sometimes it's as short as a second and sometimes it can take almost forever. Take all the time you need. When the student is ready, the breakthrough happens. There is a reason why you're reading this. Find it.

You can start at the beginning and read through to the end. Or you can start anywhere and cherry-pick the pages that most appeal to you. The book is designed to be both sequential and self-contained at the same time. Each message stands on its own but it's also integrated into the whole. I write books for people who don't have time to read. I want you to "get it" quickly and intuitively.

I want my readers to say within the first few pages, "Finally, here is a book that is going to help me to make sense of things that don't make sense to me. It's going to help me navigate my way through my future so I can make the biggest impact."

Every breakthrough has a gestation period.

Above all, this is a fun activity. It's what you do during your time off and your time on. Read it when you're fresh but also read it when you're tired. It's designed as both an inspiration and an enabler for whenever you need it.

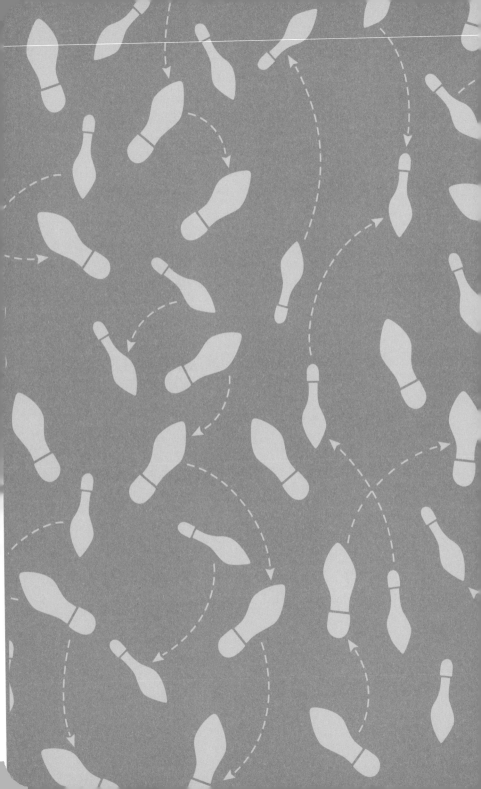

YOU HAVE TO BE A "BIT MAD" –
LIKE MACRON, VARADKAR AND BEZOS

Macron, Varadkar and Bezos epitomize
the reasons for this book. They are playing
the biggest game imaginable. They are
ambassadors of radical optimism.
They are just insane enough to believe
they can pull it off, and they can.

O N APRIL 6, 2016, Emmanuel Macron launched his new political party in France, called En Marche! (On the Move). He admitted that his mission was "a bit mad." He wanted to put an end to the stale political divide between left and right, restore national confidence and unblock France. He hadn't even turned forty and he had never run for office before; just over a year later, on May 14, 2017, he became president. At a time when democracies are being driven to extremes by doubt and pessimism, Macron has made openness to change his central platform.

The *Economist* calls it "the improbable, inescapable quest to reform France." Mr. Macron said, "Everybody told us it was impossible. But they didn't know France ... There are moments of great acceleration of history and I think we are living through one of them."

Around the same time as Macron became president of France, Leo Varadkar became prime minister of Ireland. Varadkar is the first gay man to occupy this position. At thirty-eight, he is also the youngest, and as the son of an Indian immigrant, he is also the first from an ethnic minority. Varadkar brands himself as "a champion of those who get up early in the morning."

A few days after Varadkar's victory, on the other side of the Atlantic, another extraordinary event occurred: Amazon, the online retailer, purchased Whole Foods, America's biggest premium grocer, for $13.7 billion. The deal is a transformative transaction not just for food retail, but for retail in general. Amazon acquired instant access to 460 stores selling $16 billion in high-end food. It also represents a profound shift in its attitude toward bricks-and-mortar stores.

Even restaurant operators will feel the pinch of Amazon's takeover because Whole Foods has a $3 billion restaurant business. David Palmer, retail analyst at RBC Dominion Securities, called it "a seminal moment in the world of eating."

The *New York Times* recently stated that, "unlike almost every other chief executive, Amazon's founder, Jeff Bezos, has built his company by embracing risk, ignoring obvious moves and imagining what customers want next—even before they know it. Key to that strategy is his approach to failure. While other companies dread making colossal mistakes, Mr. Bezos seems just not to care. Losing millions of dollars for some reason doesn't sting. Only success counts. That breeds a fiercely experimental culture that is disrupting entertainment, technology and, especially, retail."

As Bezos explained, "I've made billions of dollars of failures... If you're going to take bold bets, they're going to be experiments. And if they're experiments, you don't know ahead of time if they're going to work. Experiments are by their very nature prone to failure. But a few big successes compensate for dozens and dozens of things that didn't work."[1]

Macron, Varadkar and Bezos epitomize the reasons for this book. They are playing the biggest game imaginable. They are ambassadors of radical optimism. They are just insane enough to believe they can pull it off, and they are. They are amplified versions of the millions of disruptors who are reinventing their worlds in ways both big and small. Just like us, right?

A time to run toward the future

Disruption. It rhymes with destruction, followed by construction. It is a radical change that shatters the status quo. Ironically, it's the one thing you can count on. In this way, it's radical change as a constant.

No matter who we are and no matter where we live, we face a future that's nothing like our past. Every day, things are happening that rock our world or violate our values. Change is too small a word to describe the revolution we're all participating in. It's extreme. It's exhilarating. It's exhausting. No matter how inspired we are, we're going to experience moments of sheer panic—maybe multiple times a day.

In a world that seems to be spinning out of control, we need Sherpas to show us the way, help us shoulder the burden, and create safe zones where we can venture where others are afraid to go. That's the role I want to play for you. As a strategic coach and global motivator who has worked with over a million people in forty-three countries, I track the traits of highly effective disruptors. I'm always in conversations about leadership and innovation. I share perspectives for a living. I'm a cross-pollinator of potential.

Disruption can seem like incomprehensible chaos occurring with accelerating intensity. But I'm here to tell you that crises are the engines that drive transformation. They are urgent calls to action. They get us moving by making it impossible to stand still. In the face of breakdown, you—the reader—are presented with the opportunity to break through. The most powerful motivation

Paradoxically, the biggest obstacle facing people can be stability.

to find a way or make a way to succeed comes when the alternative is annihilation. Some people grab it and some don't. Some find the courage and others succumb to their fear.

Paradoxically, the biggest obstacle facing people can be stability. When things seem to be copacetic, people are reluctant to shake things up. They believe the status quo will continue. They ask, if it isn't broken, why fix it? They are lulled into a false sense of security even though they know that someone could change everything in a heartbeat. No one can awaken a person who pretends to sleep.

Understand that I'm not talking about disruption for the sake of disruption—the kind of destructive change that takes over the host like a deadly cancer. No one, except for sociopaths, wakes up intending to wreak havoc on the world. What we're talking about here is positive radicals, people who are willing to do whatever it takes, but always with a benign purpose in mind. They aren't pulled kicking and screaming into the future. They pull the future toward them. They anticipate what's coming and then move forward to meet it.

Get ready. I predict with total certainty that unprecedented crises are on their way to meet you. Like a tsunami, disruption begins long before you feel its consequences. It can be super scary. It can be overwhelming. You may just want to run away. But that's when you need to decide to run toward the future. You may not always see what you like, but you can always like what you see. You can make the shift that shapes what happens next.

It's not enough just to know what to do. You have to *do* what you know. Others are depending on it. So let's dive deep and step back at the same time in order to see the direction in which things are moving.

It's not going to get any less dangerous any time soon. After the terror attacks in Central London on June 3, 2017, London's Metropolitan Police issued a warning on social media that encapsulated the spirit of the times: "RUN—to a place of safety. This is a better option than to negotiate or surrender. If there is nowhere to go, the... HIDE—turn your phone to silent or vibrate. Barricade yourself in if you can. TELL—the police by calling 999 when it is safe to do so."[2]

That may be the safe and sane thing to do. But just like many everyday heroes, you may choose to act differently. In Jerusalem, for example, civilians are encouraged to "take action, to engage." According to the mayor, Nir Barkat, "fully one third of the 'neutralizing' of terrorists in Jerusalem is by civilians."[3]

Maybe there is no such thing as a civilian anymore, just ordinary warriors on the front lines of life.

The future belongs to those who can anticipate it

It is increasingly clear that the mind is drawn to the future, not driven by the past. We learn not by storing static records but by retouching memories and imagining future possibilities. Our emotions are less reactions to the present than guides to future behaviors. MARTIN SELIGMAN, professor of psychology, *University of Pennsylvania*

We're only as happy as what we expect to happen next. As Seligman indicates, we're meaning-making machines. We process our present environment and experiences through the filter of "what does this mean for my future and how do I prepare effectively for it?" If we believe we have the answers to those questions, we're likely to be happy. The problem arises when the velocity of change is so great that we cannot anticipate what could happen next. It's like stepping into the void, and fear of the void is the biggest fear of all.

Anything can seem like insanity if you don't understand the reasons for it. That is precisely why we begin by looking at trends. These are signals of where things are going. The more powerful the trend, the greater its influence. By understanding the trends driving disruption, you can get ahead of them. As Walt Disney said, "Find a parade and get in front of it."

I've identified these trends by interviewing hundreds of influential people and researching multiple sources through my work with Environics and the media. As you review them, think about how they are affecting you at this very moment and how you can use them to thrive in the future.

The first trend is the rise in "vital action." This is the state of being strong and active. It is the quality of personal energy. It comes from having a strong purpose and taking action to achieve it. Leaders are encouraging their communities to rise above their circumstances to create new ones. Sitting still is not an option. You cannot afford to wait and see what happens. You need to act and cause things to happen.

The second trend is the rise in intensification. Sweat the small stuff because there is no small stuff. Everything matters. Winning means getting the granular issues right. It means doing the fundamentals extraordinarily well. It demands wholehearted commitment to every endeavour every day. Every meaningful contest is being closely fought deep into overtime. Victory is being measured in inches. Emotions are embedded in every situation. Whoever shows that they want it the most wins.

The third trend is the rise in "voloptimism." This is the fusion of volatility and optimism. It means interpreting disruptive change as an opportunity to innovate and grow, not to withdraw and divorce. The winning mindset is expansionary. It's all about engagement, not withdrawal. Now is the time to reach out and touch as many people as possible, because if you don't, other winners will.

The fourth trend is the rise in transparency. Full disclosure is the only way to play. Whatever you hide will come back to haunt you. Authenticity amplifies your authority. Put it out there. If you see it, say it. Surprise people to the upside. Never let them find out what you should have told them in the first place. Trust carries a higher premium than ever before. At some point, things will go wrong. Straight talk is the only way to put them right.

The fifth trend is the rise in community alliances. The world may be full of opportunities but is also full of threats. It's going to take more than a village to triumph. It's going to take multiple communities. Winners are collaborating at a whole new level to align with like-minded stakeholders. They're constantly campaigning for the votes of the people who count. Right now I'm recruiting you to my cause so you call me, not the other guy, when you need someone to motivate and inspire your team. The time to motivate others to help you is before you need them to be motivated to help you. **The sixth trend is the rise in personalization.** Nobody wants to be one of a million. We all want to be one in a million. Winners are getting up close and personal with their customers. They are using all the available data to know more about their customers' needs and wants. Robo-advisers like Wealthsimple are building the best investment portfolios for us. Apple is curating our playlists. Amazon is anticipating our daily shopping sprees. I'm tailoring my programs specifically to the needs of each and every audience. One size fits no one. Call it mass bespoke tailoring.

The seventh trend is the rise in "true fiction." Oxford Dictionaries chose "post-truth" as its international word of the year for 2016. It defines the word as "relating to or denoting circumstances in which objective facts are less influential in shaping public opinion than appeals to emotion and personal belief." Fiction is more powerful than facts because fiction is what you do with the facts. People don't buy the truth, they buy belief. According to a study by Pew Research Center, 44 percent of us read our news on Facebook. It may be fake news, but that distinction is irrelevant to the people influenced by it. Winners tell stories in such a way that they challenge and affirm others at the same time. Just like I'm doing with you now.

The eighth trend is the rise in utility. If you want to go far, travel light. Make everything work harder for you. There is always more toothpaste in the tube. Share your assets so you can make them pay. It could be your bedroom, your car, your office, your network, your money or your time. Overheads can become get-aheads if you use them wisely. Do more with what you have. Redeploy it or get rid of it. It's the new spartanism—pare yourself down to the essentials so nothing is superfluous. If it doesn't add value or accelerate revenue, you can't afford it.

Ian Schrager has been called "the original hospitality disrupter" by *Fortune* magazine. In August 2017, he launched PUBLIC New York, a stylish 370-room luxury property on Manhattan's Lower East Side. The disruption is in the price: $150 per night. When he was asked how he managed to offer such low rates, he said, "By editing and rethinking the business model and getting rid of all those things that people really don't care about that are superfluous and leftovers from a bygone era. I don't think getting service [from] somebody in a military uniform with gold buttons and gold epaulets and white gloves, with an obsequious manner, is something that people really care about... They don't care about those traditional signposts of luxury."[4]

The ninth trend is the rise in diversity. According to Pew Research Centre, millennials are now the biggest cohort in the workplace, followed by Gen Xers and boomers. In 2018 expect to see more companies take action to ensure that more females occupy powerful positions.

Immigrants in the United States and their US-born children now number approximately 81 million people, or 26 percent of the overall US population. In 2014 alone, 1.3 million people immigrated to the United States, an 11 percent increase over the previous year. In 2016, Canada welcomed a record 321,000 new immigrants. The increase in immigration numbers is the largest in more than a century. So unleash your inner immigrant. Embrace views that are different from your own. Reflect the society you represent. Break down the barriers if you want to break through to the next level.

The final trend is the rise in "everyday heroism." The future is being created by ordinary people who take disproportionate responsibility. They have a built-in sense of accountability to do the things that need to be done. They refuse to let things slide. They speak truth to power. They have the courage and conscience to hold others to account. They also use the tools that are accessible to everyone. They are the heartbeat of any organization or community. If you are an everyday hero, I salute you. If you're not, make sure you stay very close to someone who is.

Success comes from anticipating where the opportunities are going to be and getting there first.

Deconstructing the creed of speed

Disruptors quickly learn how to ignore the many things that don't count so they can pay attention to the few that do. They know that constant pedal to the metal will only burn them out. They know when to accelerate and when to cruise.

The idea, for instance, that everything is accelerating everywhere you turn is not reality. While the metabolism of change has indeed quickened in many ways, it is also stabilizing in many others:

- New technology is spreading faster than ever, but technology companies are settling into longer-term views in terms of production as well as investment. Intel, the giant computer-chip maker, puts $20 billion a year into plant and R&D investment. Andy Bryant, Intel's chairman, states, "Our scientists have a ten-year view... If you don't take a long view it is hard to keep your production costs consistent with Moore's Law," which holds that computer processing power doubles every two years at the same cost.

- In the stock market, large "passive" fund managers such as BlackRock and Vanguard have become much bigger in the past decade and their holding periods are indefinite.
- The rate of new consumer-product launches is probably slowing or in decline. Factories do not seem to be making things faster.[5] Although we hear about new companies like Uber or Airbnb, these firms are platforms for purchasing services. Beneath them, the assets and people—cars, rooms, drivers—change far less dramatically, if at all.
- As well as lower rates of new company creation, industries have become more oligopolistic. Of thirteen industrial sectors in America, ten were more concentrated in 2007 than they had been in 1997. Since then there has been a huge round of mergers in health care, consumer goods, airlines, cable TV, telecoms and technology hardware.
- Extremely strict compliance and regulatory mandates are retarding new product and service introductions. They are also raising barriers to entry in many categories.

What is accelerating is the amount of information that we're accessing on a daily basis. So much is coming at us so fast that

Life is about luck and timing, but you can make your luck if you choose your timing.

everything appears to be accelerating frantically. We're drowning in data but we're desperate for the right knowledge and insights.

The moral of the story is this: life is about luck and timing, but you can make your luck if you choose your timing. Decide when to be proactive and when to be patient. Decide what to focus on and what to forgo. Decide when to go fast and when to go slow. Worrying about missing out because you can't do it all is only going to wear you down.

Unpacking disruption

Now that we've looked at the trends, let's consider why everyone is suddenly talking about disruption.

It was Harvard Business School professor Clayton Christensen who first linked the word "disruption" with the transformation of business models and technology. By coining the term "disruptive innovation," disruption, particularly as it relates to technology, immediately became part of our lexicon. (One researcher actually tracked the number of media articles mentioning "disruptive innovation" between 2010 and 2015 and determined an increase of almost 450 percent.*)

These days, the word "disruption" shows up daily in news articles and social media posts. It was mentioned seven times alone in one brief *Financial Post* article on June 13, 2017. It covers technology and beyond. Disruption warnings scream out from headlines: "Disruption Ahead," "Are You Prepared for Disruption," "Areas Ripe for Disruption."

---

* EY Analytics using Factiva database. Figures show number of media articles mentioning "disruptive innovation" in each calendar year, excluding duplicates.

Hollywood understands the compelling power of disruption to engage and entertain us. The top-grossing movies in 2017 include *Guardians of the Galaxy Vol. 2*, *Wonder Woman*, *Justice League* and *Spider-Man: Homecoming*, all featuring superheroes fighting evil-doers seeking mega-disruption.

Responding to disruption has also become a central issue for organizations everywhere. Even as I write these words, the City of Toronto has just announced the appointment of a Chief Resilience Officer "to meet unexpected challenge... as well as the everyday stresses facing our growing city."[6]

So what is it about disruption that both fascinates us and scares us? And, as we become more accepting of its inevitability, how can we use it to reinvent our worlds?

Disruption is given two definitions in the Merriam-Webster dictionary: 1) "to break apart, throw into disorder" and 2) "to interrupt the normal course or unity of." Random House dictionary also defines it as a "radical change in an industry, especially involving a new product or service that creates a new market."

A **disruptor**, on the other hand, is defined as someone who destroys, temporarily, the normal continuance or unity of something. A disruptor creates the conditions for something new to happen. A disruptor is also a person who precipitates a fundamental shift in thinking, action and consequences.

Disruption has evolved from being episodic to being continuous. Radical change is the new normal. It's not something that we can ever get used to. In fact, it's impossible to get used to something that's always changing. It's always going to be unsettling. We can only prepare for it as best we can, over and over again.

The four-minute mile has become the two-hour marathon

All the disruptors that I researched for this book didn't "get used to" anything. Instead they're always getting ready to be ready, whatever the challenge. They've trained their muscles to respond to their evolving environment. They keep getting better but it never gets easier. Easy isn't what they're after. Being the best, making an impact, building a following and breaking records is what they're after.

Eliud Kipchoge is an expression of this ethos. On May 6, 2017, he came agonizingly close to becoming the first person to run a marathon in under two hours when he completed the 26.2-mile course in two hours and twenty-five seconds. He was under a second per mile too slow. Together with his sponsor, Nike, Kipchoge is part of a program called Breaking2. Nike says, "Breaking2 is a quest to fully measure the extent of what the body is fully capable of. Nike is looking to push the limits of human potential through product innovation, smarter training and an optimized environment—helping our athletes run what has never been run before."

That's the goal here: to provide you with the inspiration and insights to help you achieve what you've never achieved before. The rest is up to you. So here are my questions to spark your own disruption:

- What is your personal two-hour marathon?
- What is the amazing breakthrough that is just beyond your reach?
- Who are your sponsors and partners that can help you smash through?

The deep desire for disruption

Human beings are unique in their ability and willingness to bring about change in order to improve their conditions. Researchers know that, unlike lesser primates, the human brain is able to exchange ideas with others and then elevate those concepts to a higher level. In traditions and cultures spanning thousands of years, self-improvement and community development are the two primary themes.

We have a fundamental urge to link our minds together, according to Thomas Suddendorf, an evolutionary psychologist at the University of Queensland. "This allows us to take advantage of others' experiences, reflections and imaginings to prudently guide our own behaviour."[7]

All of this means we're not content with the status quo. Human beings actually look for ways to bring about change. We're not satisfied with situations that remain static or stuck. Think of an all-inclusive resort, or perhaps Disneyworld. They are wonderful places to visit; everything is neatly organized, shiny clean and predictable. You can spend a few days there but after a certain point, you begin to crave something more. You actually want the tension, the pressure, the untidiness, the unpredictability of real life.

This is the world view of a disruptor. Yes, it can seem painful. Yes, it's disconcerting. It's disturbing. It's alarming. It's even messy. Initially, it's going to be threatening. It is an upheaval of the present and a violation of the past. Your first instinct may be to move away from it. Then you study it more closely, out of either necessity or opportunity. Now you see a whole new realm of possibility.

The view is always better when you're moving forward. We are always stronger when we trust our capacity to handle the challenge. And we always have people around us who are able and willing to step up with us. Just like you can't run away from your shadow, you can't run away from things that are here to stay. Remember, FEAR means "Face Everything And Rule."

Disruption from an intensively human point of view: Master the Six Ps

This book is not about disruption that is dominated by technology. It's about disruption that is uniquely human. Unless you're a tech company, technology is not the transformational agent—people are. Technology is their tool.

Technology enables something to be done better, more efficiently. Over 99 percent of people reading these words engage in value-adding activities that use technology but are not defined by their technology. They don't sell algorithms for a living. As Jim Collins, author of *Good to Great*, states, "When used right, technology becomes an accelerator of momentum, not a creator of it." According to Collins, research shows that while technology is important in business, it is the primary cause of neither greatness nor decline. Technology is the infrastructure that underpins one's business. If the infrastructure is obsolete, the business will follow.

This means that you must take disruption personally. You may not be able to change the entire world, but you can change your world. Your world is the space around you that includes the people you are able to touch. Your ability to change your world relies on how well you can master the "Six Ps of Disruption."

People vote with their legs—either toward you or away from you. If you find yourself on your own or isolated, it's not because others are unappreciative of you. It's because you haven't done anything that is worth appreciating. People move toward you if you represent any one of the Six Ps: **pleasure, profit, power, position, progress or protection.**

People are attracted to pleasure and allergic to pain. The greater the disruption, the greater our need for people we believe can help us through it. We can only face the future because of the people who have got our back. We go looking for them. We hear about them. We're guided by others toward them. We may even go back to them because they've been there for us in the past. They become our heroes and sheroes. We admire them for their remarkable ability to take on the challenge while they take us along with them.

So it begins with **pleasure.** Against the backdrop of tension, dread and fear, we want to feel joy. We want to be happy. We want well-being. Pleasure is the threshold that we cross to access the other five Ps.

Then it's about **profit.** As Rod Tidwell said to Jerry Maguire in the 1996 hit of the same name, "Show me the money!" If you are known as someone who makes other people money, they will forgive you for many other sins. I have worked with someone for fifteen years who has made me a huge amount of money. He is a difficult and volatile character. But he's also a genius whose contribution dwarfs any downsides of dealing with him.

There is an entire industry called "lobbying" that is about one thing: access to **power.** If you can introduce people to power, either within themselves or through powerful people, people are going to want to hang with you. That's what I'm doing here. I'm connecting you to the power within and I'm sharing how to access powerful people at the same time. Can you feel it already?

Then it's about **position.** It's about promotion and upward mobility. It's about helping others climb the ladder of success. But in order to lift others up, you must be on higher ground. You need the perspective that enables others to plan their moves. If you develop a reputation as a king-maker, kings will take very good care of you.

Then it's about **progress**. Innovation. Breakthroughs. Invention. Pioneering. Leadership. Irrespective of your domain, you'll command a premium and attract a following if you can lead progress in a desired direction. This may be the hardest way to win. It requires a creative genius and a steel will to imagine the future and then make it real. That's why the "crazy ones" are the giant legends who grow more mythical over time. Steve Jobs. Albert Einstein. Elon Musk. Thomas Edison. James Dyson. Jeff Bezos. Bill and Melinda Gates. Malala Yousafzai. Nelson Mandela. Martin Luther King. These are icons who have changed the world. But in our signature way, you and I can change our worlds. That's my dream for this book.

Finally, it's about **protection**. It's about keeping us safe from harm. It's about building walls and sustaining the infrastructure. It's about knowing someone is standing guard at the door to our homes. If others know they can depend on you in times of danger, they will move toward you in those times. And it's not going to get any less dangerous any time soon.

No matter how community- and social-minded you are, at some point disruption is going to be a very individual act. Play from your primary strength. Concentrate on an element of disruption that aligns with your skill. Care deeply about making a difference. When you consider disruption in this way, it can be entirely within your power.

Everything in this book is aimed at helping you excel on one or more of the Six Ps while you help others do the same. I have developed a followership of leaders because I've helped them thrive on one or all of the Six Ps. Think about where you can have your biggest impact and begin there.

Are you a disruptor or a disruptee?

You're either doing the disrupting or you're being disrupted. It's binary. Neutral is not a gear you can move forward in.

You are a disruptor if you:

- Love the next new thing
- Go looking for trouble because that's where the opportunities are
- Are remarkably knowledgeable about your business
- Achieve operational excellence—you know that without functional mastery, mediocrity is the most one can hope for
- Are crystal clear on your mission
- Are disproportionate in your passion
- Are willing to think big and act bold
- Act as your stakeholders' eyes and ears so they can sense what's coming next
- Always follow through—you are your word: if you say it, you do it
- Light others up, no matter what the circumstances
- Build great teams and alliances
- Always have a Plan B, and C, and D

You are a disruptee if you:

- Act with ambivalence
- Are tentative and hesitant to challenge the status quo
- Worry about looking good and what others will say
- Are satisfied with being second best
- Complain and blame others for what you believe is wrong
- Have many excuses and alibis for why it cannot be done
- Run from problems

- Use phrases like "it's not my fault" or "we've always done it like this" or "we've tried this before" or "I told you so"
- Get trapped in minutiae
- Are easily distracted and discouraged
- Quit prematurely

Become your own movement, one step at a time

No matter who you are, part of your job is to be a disruptor. In any given meeting, you can choose to be the disruptor. In fact, anyone can be a disruptor but no one can be a disruptor all the time. Choose your moments. Then go for it. The alternative is to be paralyzed—or worse, even regretful. If there is something meaningful at stake, being a disruptor is a duty.

If it doesn't feel safe to be a disruptor, then you have to calibrate the risk. You have a call to make. But you cannot just be resigned. If you are hesitant to challenge others, ask questions that test the water: Are you open to some outside-the-envelope thinking? Is it okay to challenge the status quo here? Can I propose something entirely new? Get the level of clearance before you say it. Find out if the environment is open to a comment. Challenge without

The mythology of disruption involves taking on the monster.

threatening. You'll be surprised at the number of people who were waiting for someone to ask what you asked or say what you said.

If you are going to be a disruptor, you go where others are afraid to go. The mythology of disruption involves taking on the monster. It entails coming face to face with the ogre, the dragon, the troll, the beast or the barbarian. Every success story has confrontation with a nemesis wrapped up in it. Most of the time the nemesis is both internal and external. Conquer the one and you'll conquer the other. It's never going to be comfortable, but then comfort leads to inertia. So be comfortable being uncomfortable.

As a disruptor, your number one fear will be figuring out how to do something you've *never* done before. The odds will always be against you—at the beginning. You see things that no one has seen. You feel a power and excitement that no one else feels. At first, you may appear to others as a modern-day madman. Then you build your case. You attract like-minded warriors and game-changers to your cause. You achieve small wins. Colleague by colleague, customer by customer, you build your scale. Then, one day, you cross the threshold of experimentation into full-blooded success. And that's when the challenges really begin.

There's no disruption until someone is willing to be visible. What will that take? How can you *adapt, navigate* and *pivot* in a way that *inspires, delights* and *thrills* others? How can you build the stamina and tenacity to become unstoppable? How can you find the breakthrough that is so compelling it's worthy of your life?

You gotta love the sweat: Motivation equals prize minus pain

Disruption appears to outside observers as a sudden breakthrough. The truth is that it is an excruciating *grind*. The "big idea" is never a big idea at the time. It is the seed of a possibility that requires obsessive tending in order to flower.

It takes discipline, but you have to infuse it with inspiration. The reward must be greater than the pain of earning it. Motivation equals prize minus pain. The joy of achievement must override the agony of the struggle. Other people are amazed by your results because they don't see the grit and guts that make the impossible possible.

There are also times when you can relax and recharge. You can enjoy the ride. You can count on timeless rhythms repeating themselves. Winning is not about changing for the sake of change. It's about understanding the ebb and flow of your industry and catching the wave just before it breaks, over and over again. There is a time to paddle furiously and there is a time to sit, watch and dream. You have to know when to do what.

Avoidance is not an option

Trying to avoid disruption is like trying to defy gravity. You're going to fall on your ass. If you think it can never happen where you live or work, you're in for a guaranteed shock. Expect disruption to impact your life today. Act as though it will. Be productively paranoid. You don't know exactly when it will happen, but you do know it will definitely happen. Avoidance is a recipe for mediocrity

> **Avoidance is a recipe for mediocrity and defeat.**

and defeat. There is always a moment when one has to step in and step up. That moment may come sooner than you think. It always does.

If you're still contemplating avoidance, consider the following:

- Trying to avoid disruption means giving up the right to lead. It means hoping someone else becomes the leader.
- The delay is directly proportional to the extra price you are going to pay in time, effort or money to catch up. Procrastination is costly.
- Trying to avoid disruption makes you a bystander who is not in the game, so you don't even stand a chance of being a champion.
- Trying to avoid disruption makes you obsolete while it strengthens your competitors.
- Being the disruptor is hard work but it is the ticket to the show. Being the disruptee means taking multiple hits every day and being miserable. It's your choice.

How do some people make it look so easy when you know it's so hard?

You know the kind of person I'm talking about. They touch the ground lightly. They make all the right moves while they move others into action. They set the standard and make everyone else strive to meet it. They handle adversity with aplomb. When they're around, you know everything is going to work out just the way you want it to. They make the difference that you want to be a part of. They inspire while they innovate. It's a kind of magic but it's also an acquired skill.

I'm in a unique position to identify and study these people. I'm a coach and commentator who patrols the sidelines while I study the game. I look. I listen. I learn. As the great Yogi Berra said, "You can see a lot by observing." I'm fascinated by these disruptors and I've turned my fascination into this book.

No matter what their game, disruptors dance their way through it. Dancing is something that you do when you're happy or having fun. It literally means moving your body rhythmically in a pattern of steps, especially to the accompaniment of music. It also means shifting nimbly or quickly. It requires partnering with others in some kind of performance.

When you dance with someone or something, it means you're in harmony with them. You share a common purpose. You're a source of each other's joy. You're connected. You're in celebration mode. You're cognizant of your gifts. You're acutely aware of each other's actions and effect on each other. In other words, dancing is a fabulous thing to do, no matter what the circumstances.

Learning to dance with disruption means knowing what to focus on to get right, right now—with ease, calm, flexibility, determination, individuality and grace.

Think about the successful disruptors around you. Think about their way of being with others. I'll bet they all have a signature style that others find attractive. They've become a source of others' dreams and delight. They work very hard at making it look very easy. They've discovered how to dance with their environment.

Are you a source of others' joy and delight? Do others want to dance with you?

Fred Astaire, perhaps the greatest dancer of the twentieth century, described his philosophy of dancing in a way that encapsulates the key message of this book. If you take away only Astaire's insights, you'll thrive:

- "The higher up you go, the more mistakes you are allowed. Right at the top, if you make enough of them, it's considered to be your style."
- "Cultivate flexibility. Be able to adapt your style to that of your partner. In doing so, you are not surrendering your individuality, but blending it with that of your partner."
- "If it doesn't look easy, it is that we have not tried hard enough yet."
- "When you're experimenting, you have to try so many things before you choose what you want, and you may go days getting nothing but exhaustion."
- "It takes time to get a dance right, to create something memorable."

Misty Copeland, the first African-American principal ballet dancer in American Ballet Theatre history, describes her dance philosophy exquisitely:

- "There are no taking days off. There are no distractions. If I had that, I physically wouldn't be capable of going onstage and performing live theater. It's extremely demanding. I have to be in ballet class every day."
- "If the rhythm or beat of the music changes with a live orchestra, you have to think on your feet. If you feel like you are not on your leg, you have to make a decision to make it look as though nothing is going wrong."

- "I say over and over again that I am just standing on the shoulders of so many who have set this path for me, and they may not be seen or recognized or have been given an opportunity to have a voice, but I'm here representing all of those dancers. Dance Theatre of Harlem, Virginia Johnson, Tai Jimenez, Lauren Anderson."

Fred Astaire and Misty Copeland chose to literally dance for a living. The kind of dancing we're talking about here is the figurative kind. It's the expression of your unique style. It's demonstrating how much you love what you do and how brilliant you are at doing it. It's all the right moves that you make to make the best want to partner with you.

It always begins with a struggle— then you discover the secrets and it turns into a dance

Nothing is easy at the beginning. The steps are awkward and even confusing. The movement seems strange. The choreography may not even be clear. You certainly don't look graceful or elegant. You slip, trip and flip your way forward. But if you stay with it, if you commit to being someone who dances with disruption, you'll find your own way there.

Together with my fellow wizards in the Environics Group, I have discovered the seven secrets to thriving on massive change so the best people want to partner with you. A secret is a formula or knowledge that is only known to a few. It is an insight that is hidden from public view. It is a clue to success that only the astute can discern.

Secrets are valuable because they unlock the potential of other people's futures. They are crucial pieces of the puzzle that other people are trying to construct. If you can share your secrets with others in such a way that you enable their success, you'll be very valuable to them. I know. I trade in secrets. Some of them I have within me. And some of them I liberate within others.

I'm going to share with you the seven secrets that will enable you to thrive on change and attract the best people to you. The secrets are simple but they're not easy. Here is the common denominator running through all of them: look like you're enjoying yourself because you're confident in the outcome. Great dancers always have a smile on their face. They move with poise and certainty because they appear to know exactly what the next steps are, even if they don't.

The greater the disruption, the greater our need for people we believe can help us through it. The seven secrets will help you become one of those people.

BECOME
THE PERSON
WHO REALLY
KNOWS

The difference between someone who

really knows and someone who doesn't is the

willingness to do the work, find the information,

talk to the people and formulate a strategy.

The data has been democratized. Everything is out

there if you're willing to search for it. The tiniest

details can reveal the greatest insights.

But you must understand and communicate

the facts—not the alternate facts.

L ET ME BEGIN with a story about my client, Susan. Susan is a senior leader of an international multi-billion-dollar manufacturing company based in Europe. She is about to take over a major part of the global business. Susan has all the right attributes—she is savvy, personable, professional and experienced. But what really sets Susan apart is her willingness to thrust herself into the business so she understands it at the most basic level. She understands that the front line is the key to the bottom line. She is a detective of reality while she visualizes possibility.

Then Susan calls it the way she sees it. She communicates her perceptions in a direct, easy-to-understand way. She has built a reputation as someone who talks straight about things she really knows. That's why people listen to her. And that's how she is championing disruption within her organization. Her authenticity shines through.

Susan's colleagues know they can trust her as a bearer of genuine insights. She talks the talk of the front line while she demonstrates her grasp of the strategic issues. She makes the abstract concrete through her ability to turn truth into a competitive advantage.

Now pause for a moment and think about the people to whom you turn for guidance and leadership. Who are the people you trust the most to help you in crucial situations? What do they do that others don't do? How do they act? How do they think? In every case, they will be people who demonstrate a mastery of the minutiae. They will be able to zoom into the smallest details and then zoom out to the zeitgeist. "Zeitgeist" is a German word that means "spirit of the times." When someone is tuned into the zeitgeist, they develop a sixth sense of what is about to happen. But they are always rooted in the fundamentals.

Michael Adams is the founder of the Environics Research Group, one of Canada's leading research and polling companies. He is also my business partner. I chose Michael as my business partner in 2001 because he demonstrated such an acute understanding of the Canadian psyche. Michael brands himself as an environmental scanner. Over the past thirty years, he has interviewed, polled and studied more Canadians than anyone else in the country. Today, at the age of 70, he is still deeply involved in the design and administration of Environics's social values research. In 2016 he was admitted to the Order of Canada for his contribution to the field.

You can't fake genuine knowledge. You may be able to fool some of the people some of the time. But when they discover they've been had, they'll become your biggest detractors. At the same time, there is a power that comes with really knowing. And the more things change, the more they stay the same.

In Toronto, in the early 1900s, Edmund Burke designed the beautiful concrete-steel arch bridge that stretched 494 metres across the Don Valley. The bridge was controversial at the time, particularly because Burke insisted on designing in a lower deck for future mass transit. Even though streetcars were relatively new in 1900, Burke could see that in the future the growing city would be crisscrossed by some kind of modern transit system. Despite numerous public protests, Burke received the support of R. C. Harris, the powerful commissioner of public works, and the Prince Edward Viaduct was completed in 1918. Fifty-one years later, when Toronto's main east-west subway line was opened, the lower deck easily accommodated the new line without massive renovations. Burke's ability to see the future by understanding a reality that was already being transformed literally saved the Toronto Transit Commission millions of dollars.[1]

Susan, Adams, Burke and others like them are people who are able to precipitate fundamental shifts in thinking because they really know what's going on and they have the capacity to communicate their knowledge in a compelling way. They are willing to share their secrets with others. They understand that knowledge is power only if it's shared effectively.

Authentic knowledge

The person who really knows understands that secrets are everywhere—hiding in plain sight. The data is out there if you're curious enough to search for it. It's a question of priorities. You have to be willing to invest the time to talk to the people, read the publications, and go there yourself. There is no lazy man's way to becoming the person who really knows.

As noted in the *Economist* several years ago,[2] this ethos is epitomized by genchi genbutsu, a central principle of Japanese leadership philosophy. It means "go and see for yourself." It's as much an attitude as an action, and demands an on-the-ground understanding of the fundamental realities. Unless you've actually been to the site or immersed yourself in the situation at some point, you cannot expect to make optimal decisions.

Genchi genbutsu sounds lot like "get your boots on," which is exactly what you need to do. The secrets of success will not give themselves up to you if you stay in your office. You gotta go where the action is.

Again, according to Economist, "Another Japanese word, gemba, is allied to the same concept. Gemba means 'place,' the place (as it were) where the action happens. Genchi genbutsu involves going to the gemba to check on the genbutsu (the relevant objects)."[3]

Toyota is one of the fiercest devotees of genchi genbutsu. Their gemba is any road that their vehicles will travel on. As the *Economist* described, citing a story in the *Chicago Sun-Times* from February 24, 2003, "Yuji Yokoya, a Toyota engineer, was given responsibility for re-engineering a new generation of the Toyota Sienna minivan for the North American market. So he drove one more than 53,000 miles across America, from Anchorage to the Mexican border and from Florida to California."

The *Chicago Sun-Times* continued: "Crossing the Mississippi River by bridge, [Yokoya] noted that the Sienna's crosswind stability needed improvement. He observed excessive steering drift while traversing gravel roads in Alaska, and the need for a tighter turning radius along the crowded streets in Santa Fe. Driving through Glacier National Park, he decided the handling needed

Authentic knowledge is the difference between talking in clichés and persuading with power.

to be crisper. He also made an all-wheel-drive option a priority, along with more interior space and cargo flexibility."

Finally, Yokoya decided that the new Sienna would have to be a minivan that families, and especially kids, could live in for extended periods of time. Upgrading seat quality became a priority, along with "kid-friendly" features such as a roll-down window for second-row passengers, an optional DVD entertainment centre, and a conversation mirror so parents could monitor what was going on in the back seat.

The Sienna was the top-selling minivan in the United States in 2016. That might never have happened if not for Yokoya's diligence. Not everyone can travel 53,000 miles to find the truth, but we can all go the extra mile to discern the difference between authentic knowledge and noise that masquerades as knowledge.

My secret sauce as a speaker is the willingness to conduct my own genchi genbutsu. I interview star performers on my clients' teams before every session. I reference them by name. I even ask them to contribute to the session. I leverage the knowledge they have shared with me. Authentic knowledge is the difference between talking in clichés and persuading with power. What are you doing?

Mastering knowledge methodically

Knowledge mastery isn't a random activity. There are just the facts and there are the facts that matter. A lot of knowledge isn't knowledge at all; it's just information disguised as something more important. I'm talking about idle gossip, bland conversation, uninformed analysis and generalized speculation. There are many times when it is satisfying, even relaxing, to be entertained by this kind of information. We all need it as part of our "play" time. But a disruptor is one who knows the difference between trivial knowledge and relevant knowledge. The one is light and fluffy, the other pithy and probing.

Methodical knowledge mastery requires three key perspectives: the environment, the customer and oneself. Each is a blend of art and science, requiring at times left-brain analysis and logic, at other times right-brain intuition and creativity. Let's look at each separately.

Knowing the environment: Staying in front of the parade

Read 500 pages a day. That's how knowledge works. It builds up like compound interest.

WARREN BUFFET

The person who really knows is plugged into the environmental factors shaping their industry. They study the GEIST trends—Governmental, Economic, Industry, Social and Technological trends. They tune into these trends so they can get ahead of them. They make the investment of time, money and effort. And they reap the dividends.

Those who really know recognize others who really know. They also recognize those who only pretend to know. When you listen to someone who really knows, the impact is enormously reassuring. You give that person your attention because they will give a high ROA—Return On Attention. What would I think and feel if I were to listen to you? Educate first, then sell.

Governmental trends

What are the regulatory changes impacting your industry? What direction is legislation moving toward in your industry? Who are the people you should be talking to? What data should you be studying? What do you need to be sharing with your clients? Who represents your constituency in parliament?

At every conference I attend, delegates are most interested in hearing about government intentions and likely next steps. We're all subject to the law, which is why the law is such a fascinating subject. How knowledgeable are you on the law? Legislation can redefine your business overnight. Be ready or be ruined.

Economic trends

The economist is the new fortune-teller. Although no one can predict the future, the best economists sound like they can. They turn their data into "anecdata"—fact-based stories that captivate audiences. Everyone wants a glimpse into the future so they can take the right action.

My personal go-to guy is David Rosenberg, chief economist at Gluskin Sheff + Associates, a highly respected Toronto-based money management company. Rosenberg publishes a daily newsletter called *Breakfast with Dave* that is breathtaking in its scope and sheer readability. I have made key decisions and recommendations based on Rosenberg's insights, and I haven't been disappointed yet.

Economic trends provide the context in which all our decisions are made. If you are ignorant of the trends, you're flying blind. If you cannot articulate the trends impacting your industry, other people will doubt your ability to give them what they want.

So who is your source of economic insight? How informed are you on the key vectors? How familiar are you with real-time developments? How frequently are you absorbing the data? How good are you at communicating the trends in a way that convinces others that you are the person who really knows?

If you are ignorant of

the trends, you're flying

blind. If you cannot

articulate the trends impacting

your industry, other

people will doubt your ability

to give them what they want.

Industry trends

What are the specific forces redefining your marketplace? Who are the new entrants? What are they doing differently? What are your competitors doing that you wish you had done? What do your customers really want from you? How are their needs changing? What sources are you accessing to become a thought leader?

Knowledge is a highly perishable resource. It needs to be replenished multiple times a day. To have knowledge mastery, you need to keep increasing what you know every day. Within your industry, this involves talking, listening, reading, watching, writing—whatever it takes to acquire knowledge and then share your knowledge with others. It entails reading magazines, newsletters and journals, signing up for podcasts, watching videos, listening to audiobooks, talking to those who really know, exploring your company's data sources, going to industry meetings.

I spend 80 percent of my time in conversation with others. My best investment is my Starbucks card. It's amazing how much great information a great cup of coffee can get you. But first, you need to earn others' time. If you're valuable to people who are valuable to you, they'll invest time with you.

How robust is your social network? The person with the largest network wins. Some of my most powerful insights come from people at the outer edges of my network. They are the ones who are seeing things that I could never see. I meet them at conferences or engage with them online. A single thought can spark a major breakthrough. This book is the result of a conversation that I had with Bryce Moloney, senior vice president Learning and Development Division at Speakers' Spotlight, Canada's leading speakers' bureau. Bryce shared the urgency of helping organizations manage disruption in a way that enhances the well-being of their people. That's the genesis of *Dancing with Disruption*.

It's not enough just to download information. You need to upload it as well. You need to generate content, just like I'm doing here. Just as you need to consume other people's ideas, they need to consume yours. The most powerful way to learn is to define and express your own thoughts. You'll discover they're just as powerful as anyone else's. Use the Internet as your megaphone to the world. Simply expressing a point of view will differentiate you from the crowd.

What are you sending to your network on a regular basis through LinkedIn or your preferred social media channels? Build your presence and it will be reciprocated.

Your own organization can also be a source of great opportunity. The person who really knows is the one who is connecting with their colleagues and exchanging insights with them. They've found a way to use their knowledge to bring people together and make things happen. They bust bureaucracy and break down silos. They build followership by leading first. Are you? How can you foster a collaborative and open environment? How much time are you investing in building your network within the organization? How much time should you be investing?

Social trends

What are the lifestyle changes disrupting your world? What do people want most from their communities? How are their values changing? Everything is interdependent. There are no silos in real life, just one big dynamic ecosystem.

Teddy Langschmidt is an acclaimed social researcher based in Toronto. In 2017, he conducted his "Value of Values" survey of 4,500 respondents across North America. He discovered that there are ten experiences that people desire most (I resonated strongly with each one). If you can help people achieve one or more of these experiences, you'll become valuable to them:

1. Ending our unease and discomfort—We want to achieve a level of well-being in the current climate of disruption and volatility.
2. Overcoming our weaknesses—We want to feel stronger and smarter in the face of huge challenges.
3. Getting back our self-respect and self-worth—We want to experience the wins and triumphs that validate and vindicate our merit.
4. Discovering what we were meant to do—We want a sense of meaning and direction that will in turn provide a sense of completion and fulfillment.
5. Regaining control of our life—We want to feel like we're driving our own life, not being dragged along by forces beyond our control.
6. Raising our standard of living—We want to enjoy the promises of life and provide our loved ones with plenty. That's the Canadian and American Dream: to afford the pursuit of happiness.
7. Leading healthy lives—We want to be free of illness, pain and disease until the very end.
8. Guiding, leading and inspiring others—At our core, we all want to make others happy. No one, except for the truly malicious, wakes up intending to make others miserable.
9. Being experts in our field—We all want to achieve a level of mastery that enables us to do our jobs well. We also want the kudos that comes with being recognized as great at what we do.
10. Reducing our stress levels—We want to be free of worry about actual or potential problems. "Stress" is really a code word for fear. When we say we're stressed, we're really afraid of what could happen next.

Those who really know are finely tuned to the emotional values of those around them. Think of Brené Brown, a research professor of social work at the University of Houston. Brown spent years studying the factors that interfere with human connections, in particular shame and fear. After years of poring over collected data, she came to the conclusion that one of the ways to address the unease and discomfort that seem to dominate our emotions in the twenty-first century is to encourage people to embrace vulnerability instead of trying to avoid it.

Brown was unknown outside her own workplace until she presented a TED Talk and shared her knowledge with millions around the world. Her message resonated so directly with people's emotional values that her presentation quickly became one of the most watched TED Talks of all time, with over thirty million views by 2017.

No matter what industry you're in, you are dealing with people who are struggling with unprecedented fear, anxiety and fatigue. Like Brown, when you are able to find a way to address these emotional values, you are able to resonate strongly with your stakeholders. This is tantamount to being someone who really knows.

Technological trends

Someone, somewhere, is reinventing the way you sell your service and serve your clients right now. They're making it better, faster, smoother. There's always a new app for that. Are you leveraging technology to maximize your impact? Are you seen as a market innovator? Are you ahead of the technological curve? Or are your competitors making you look slow?

We're all being evaluated against the genius of Amazon, Apple or Alphabet. We can even use these titans to serve our stakeholders more effectively. All three brands are an integral part of my delivery system. I'm selling this book through Amazon in many different forms—audible, digital and analog. I'm creating the content on Apple and I'm marketing it through Google and YouTube. And yet I'm still alarmed that I'm lagging behind the technology available to me. But so is everyone. There are very few companies that are certain they are cutting-edge.

Like Sisyphus pushing the rock uphill only to have it fall down on him over and over again, we're all perennial trial-and-error explorers in this brave new world. We need partners who understand the shifts and empower us with the innovations we need to pursue our own disruptions.

As we search for the next, new, big thing, we need to remember that some of the most disruptive inventions have been cheap, simple and easy to overlook. Tim Harford recently wrote in the *Financial Times* about the "toilet paper principle," referring to the "too cheap to remark on" inventions that hide in plain sight but reorder everything. Barbed wire is another example. It enabled settlers to fence vast areas of prairie cheaply, and "once settlers could assert control over their land, they had the incentive to invest in and improve it." The corrugated steel box, 8 feet wide and 8.5 feet high and 40 feet long, is another technological disruption, Harford writes, that has streamlined and enabled shipping on an unprecedented level and accelerated the globalization of world trade.[4]

The primary question we need to ask ourselves is whether technology can do what we do better than we can do it? At the high end, the answer is no. No computer can write a book like Stephen King, dance like Misty Copeland or invest like Warren Buffet. At the low end, no computer can scrub a toilet or change the bed linens. In between, though, beware. Artificial intelligence is usurping authentic intelligence wherever it can.

Knowing your customers: The first step in the journey of disruption

As a disruptor, your mission is to win, keep and grow the most desirable customers through the breakthrough results you deliver for them. You can only execute this mission if you become an "inside-outsider." That's when you understand your customers so intimately that they bring you into their inner circle. They make you an honorary team member because they believe that you really, really appreciate the essence of their business. That's when they trust you enough to embark on the journey of disruption with you.

Here are the ten criteria that comprise a customer inside-outsider mindset—ask yourself how informed you are on each one of them:

1. I understand my customers' business models: I know how they monetize their desired outcome.
2. I know the individual decision-makers and what motivates them.
3. I know what's important to my customers beyond the scope of my interactions with them.
4. I know the politics of my customers' organizations, their culture and their language.
5. I know the influencers within my customers' organizations and their commitment to my role: I know the detractors (those who don't believe in me) and the advocates (those who do believe in me)
6. I know the current performance of my customers—top line and bottom line, inside and out.
7. I know the history of my customers' past successes and failures.
8. I know which competitors are working with my customers and how well they're doing.
9. I connect my customers to insights and breakthroughs they would not have found on their own.

10. I am spending the right amount of time with my customers to sustain my value to them.

Mastering yourself: Be always new

Mastering others is strength. Mastering yourself is true power.
LAO TSU

You're plugged into the zeitgeist and you really know your customers. Now the questions are, Do you really know yourself? Do you rule yourself? Or are you ruled by yourself? Our biggest challenge is self-mastery. So when you look at yourself in the mirror, what do you see? Is it someone you love and admire? Is it someone you wish weren't there? Or is it simply someone who has become boring?

As described by the Harvard Business Review, John W. Gardner was a legendary public intellectual, civic reformer and celebrated Stanford professor. On November 10, 1990, he delivered a famous speech to a meeting of ambitious strategists at McKinsey & Company. A man clearly committed to lifelong learning, Gardner spoke about "personal renewal." He urged leaders who wish to make a difference and stay effective to commit themselves to continued learning and exploration.

"We have to face the fact that most men and women out there in the world of work are more stale than they know, more bored

When you look at yourself in the mirror, what do you see?

than they would care to admit," he said. "Boredom is the secret ailment of large-scale organizations."

Gardner went on to describe what was far more important than the attributes typically embraced by business leaders: "[It's] not anything as narrow as ambition," Gardner said. "After all, ambition eventually wears out and probably should. But you can keep your zest until the day you die."

"Be interested," he urged. "Everyone wants to be interesting, but the vitalizing thing is to be interested... As the proverb says, 'It's what you learn after you know it all that counts.'"[5]

Curiosity is the antidote to boredom. Every day is a new opportunity for you to recreate yourself in some way. I study great motivators, interviewers, leaders and coaches to learn how they've achieved pre-eminence. I read, I travel, I write, I listen, I share what I've learned with whoever I can. I'm a student of the street. I find everything fascinating. I'm curious: how are you keeping interested? Remember: if you want to be interesting to people, be interested in them and their lives.

By doing something new, or experiencing something you've never done before, you animate your life force. You sustain your joie de vivre. By getting out of your comfort zone, you expand your capacity to create remarkable results. All the magic is beyond where you've ever been before. Think about the last time you travelled to a new destination. Think about the thrill of being in a strange new world. Now think about what you need to do to experience that thrill without leaving home. See your world through fresh eyes and you'll see a lot more than you did before.

I have been living in my adopted city of Toronto since 2001, but I make a point of looking at everything as though I've just arrived. I intentionally simulate the excitement and the joy of arriving in Canada. The result is often miraculous. I look at people as though they're a gift, and they return the sentiment.

> **Take the everyday self-renewal challenge**
> Do something you've never done.
> Be fascinated by something or someone that frustrates you.
> Appreciate something or someone that you've taken for granted.
> Talk to someone that you find exciting.
> Read or listen to something that inspires you.

Creating a personal brand that sticks: Really know what you stand for

We are living in an escalating swirl of noise and distraction. Unless we build a powerful personal brand, it's easy to be invisible or forgotten. A powerful personal brand is one that is meaningful, inspiring and differentiated from the competition. Defining your personal brand also gives you a clear sense of what you want to stand for.

Jeff Bezos, founder of Amazon, defines a personal brand perfectly: "Your brand is what people say about you when you're not in the room."

So what do you want others to be saying about you when you're not in the room? It's not good enough to want to stand for excellence, integrity, honesty, professionalism, trustworthiness, experience, and so on. Those qualities are table stakes. They're expected. You need to define your personal brand in a way that conveys your unique value to your stakeholders.

In my case, I want to be seen as someone "who excites others into powerful action that achieves unprecedented results." I want to be a catalyst for other people's development. I want people to see me as co-pilot on their journey of life. Often my ability to express my personal brand in a succinct phrase wins me the business in a tight race. It's the final deposit that tilts the scales in my favour.

Whenever I complete this exercise with delegates, they struggle initially with a "personal brand statement." Then they unleash their creativity and have fun. Here are some of the statements I've heard:

- I'm a master organizer with an eye for the tiniest detail.
- I'm a no-limits marketing guru who will turn you into a selling machine.
- I'm an Excel god who can tame the numbers through any spreadsheet.
- I'm a financial matchmaker who can introduce you to the real money.
- I'm a charismatic connector who brings people together to form world champion teams.

Oprah Winfrey defined her personal brand as, "To be a teacher. And to be known for inspiring my students to be more than they thought they could be." Denise Morrison, CEO of Campbell Soup Company, defines her brand as, "To serve as a leader, live a balanced life and apply ethical principles to make a significant difference."

When you know what you stand for, you can take a stand in every part of your life. As someone "who excites others into powerful action that achieves unprecedented results," I have to be that person. I have to manifest that mission. I can't be wishy-washy. Wimping out is never an option. It simplifies my way forward. I am often wrong, but I'm never in doubt.

Setting your one most important goal: Really know *what* you want to achieve

An old Chinese saying states, "The man who chases two chickens catches neither."

I often ask people what is the one most important goal that they want to achieve in the next year. They struggle with their response. The most common response is that they have many goals that are blurred in their mind. They kind-of, sort-of, more-or-less know their goals. But they can't declare the primary goal that inspires them to achieve all others.

Disruptors have a vision, not double vision. They have a very clear goal that inspires them to inspire others to help them achieve their goal. Here's mine: "I want to create a million disruptors through this book over the next year." If I achieve that goal, everything else will follow—the revenue, the speaking engagements, the kudos and the self-actualization. I can see a million people disrupting the world to the benefit of the other 7.5 billion people on the planet.

What can you see? Don't be modest in your goal-setting. The poet Robert Browning wrote, "Ah, but a man's reach should exceed his grasp / Or what's a heaven for?" Write down your primary goal. Stretch it. Then commit to it.

Once you set your primary goal, you can help other people set theirs. Disruption is a function of how effectively you can get people to believe in their primary goals. All the disruptors I discuss in this book enabled their stakeholders to believe in an expanded primary goal that spurred them into action.

As a disruptor, what is your primary goal that will inspire you to inspire others?

Set your strategy: Really know how you're going to achieve your goal

Strategy is defined as "a method for achieving consistent success." It's a way of thinking and acting that delivers your desired results. Your strategy can evolve over time in response to changing circumstances.

The best strategies can be expressed in a single sentence. In fact, if you cannot express your strategy in a single sentence, you don't have a strategy. Here are some extraordinary examples:

- "Inspire and nurture the human spirit—one person, one cup and one neighborhood at a time" (Starbucks)
- "Bring inspiration and innovation to every athlete* in the world" (Nike
- "Create an unrivaled environment for exceptional people" (McKinsey & Company)

---

* The legendary University of Oregon track and field coach, and Nike co-founder, Bill Bowerman said, 'If you have a body, you are an athlete.'

- "No more waiting. No more watching on a schedule that's not your own. No more frustration. Just Netflix how, when and wherever you are in the world" (Netflix)
- "We are Ladies and Gentlemen serving Ladies and Gentlemen" (The Ritz-Carlton)

I sell motivation for a living. My clients may be running on empty or they may just need a top-up. Either way, I need to infuse them with the energy and excitement they need to get their motor running. My strategy, therefore, is to "be excited in order to excite others."

By setting out my strategy, I'm compelled to interpret everything around me as raw material for creating this excitement. When things are copacetic, it's easy. When things are crazy, I get creative about how I spin my circumstances to extract the right meaning.

My strategy is conscious. It informs my actions. It makes me intentional in my actions. I'm aware of when I'm executing my strategy and when I'm not. It's the difference between reaching my goals and going nowhere.

What's more, when you share your strategy with others, it gives them a sense of confidence in you. It's so rare that people have a conscious personal strategy that they can articulate to others. Simply expressing it will set you apart from the crowd.

Write down, in a single phrase, the strategy that has got you to this point. Is it working for you? Does it inspire and enable you to be remarkable? Or is it time to formulate a new strategy?

When you're causing disruption, you're going to be encountering multiple surprises all the time.

Taking action: Really know your daily plan of action

We all know people who tell us what they are "going to do." They make promises they don't keep or commitments they don't honour. They talk big but they don't follow through. Their actions are inconsistent—sometimes they're awesome and other times they're not.

Disruptors are people of action. They see the opportunity and they go for it. They know that every day is our life in miniature. They know that what they do on any day can influence every other day. They keep moving forward. They know that action is how they strengthen their mental muscles to take on tougher and bigger tasks. But it isn't frenetic action. It's a daily plan of action focused on their primary goal and guided by their strategy.

Your daily plan of action is a set of concerted actions that you take continuously to move forward. This isn't just a "to do" list. It is a discipline that you practise every single day. It's non-negotiable. The more you do it, the better you become—just like a surgeon who performs an operation daily is going to be a lot more proficient than one who only performs it weekly.

When you're causing disruption, you're going to be encountering multiple surprises all the time. You're going to be dealing with other people's anxieties and fears. Your daily plan of action is the platform that gives you the certainty to lead.

My plan of action is:

1. Learn and grow through reading, listening and writing.
2. Enhance my physical vitality through the right exercise and diet.
3. Give generously to others before I need anything from them.
4. Strengthen my network by talking to others in person, on the phone and online.
5. Relax, play and have fun.

Once you commit to a daily plan of action, you give up your alibis. You hold yourself accountable to yourself. There is no easy exit. You say what you'll do and you do what you say. You become known as the kind of person who can be trusted in all seasons.

What is your daily plan of action that will enable you to rise above your alibis?

Staying in the know

Be warned. There is a lot of alone time required in handling disruption. One needs the silence of solitude to curate and create new ideas. The mind, however, can be a nerve-racking place. It often makes us scared to explore our thoughts. We never know where they're going to take us. Sometimes it feels like they're impossible to control. But disruptors need to make time to process their thinking and alchemize their breakthroughs—just like I'm doing now.

At some point, someone has to distill the essence of all the conversation and idea-exchange. That person needs to be you if you're taking on the responsibility of being a disruptor. It always takes more time than you think, especially when you don't think that you have the time. But find the time you must. Otherwise the swirl will just sweep you along.

As a rule of thumb, you should be spending at least 20 percent of your time thinking about how you can positively disrupt your business. That's at least eight to ten hours a week. You'll discover that 20 percent multiplies the impact of the other 80 percent.

Choose the game-changing issues that are transforming your world and then dance with them to the sound of your own music. Look at them from multiple angles. Express yourself by writing your thoughts down. When you're ready, share them with others.

Whenever I invest time in creating a new program or book, I'm always sharper afterwards. I've done the heavy lifting so I have a stronger grasp of the issues. It always pays dividends, including the words you're reading now.

Applauding yourself

No one ever gets enough kudos, love or appreciation. Admiration is the ultimate aphrodisiac. That's why the best disruptors are always celebrating highly productive people, including themselves. Catch yourself doing something right. Reward yourself with a bonus in the form of whatever turns you on.

In my case, whenever I win a great engagement or create a new breakthrough, I take the time to applaud myself with a pause, a micro-treat such as a latte or a fine wine. If it's really significant, it means an evening out, a special purchase or a weekend away.

Each of us is both a performer in our area of expertise and an individual with varying degrees of doubt and angst. Sometimes other people congratulate us, and other times we need to do the

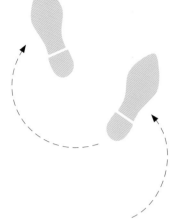

Disruptors share, not hoard.

There's no return in being

stingy with your know-how.

I've never regretted being

generous. I've always

regretted not being

generous enough.

job ourselves. You're not crazy if you laugh and smile to yourself. You're simply acknowledging that you're willing to take on the tough issues and go through the grind of moving forward. Enjoy.

Paying it forward

Don't judge each day by the harvest you reap but by the seeds that you plant.

ROBERT LOUIS STEVENSON

Just as you rely on others to help you become one who really knows, they're relying on you. Sometimes they'll reach out to you with a specific request, and sometimes you need to proactively include them in the know. Disruptors share, not hoard. There's no return in being stingy with your know-how. I've never regretted being generous. I've always regretted not being generous enough.

I'm generous not because I'm a good Samaritan. I give to get. The most valuable currency in a relationship-driven marketplace is reciprocity. I know that at some point, when I need it most, my generosity will be repaid. Now is always the time to give as much as you can. Trust me—you'll need the dividends when they come. The hallmark of outstanding performers is that they constantly build a pipeline of potential that rewards them at a future point.

At least 70 percent of my work is the result of someone calling me as a result of a contribution I've made, directly or indirectly, to their success. It could have been a personal conversation, a presentation, a video, a blog or a book. The point is that they see me as someone who really knows how to help them really know. How many people have you helped today?

Final thought: Know that you know and keep learning more

Some are born great, some achieve greatness, and others have greatness thrust upon them.

TWELFTH NIGHT, act 2, scene 5

In *Twelfth Night*, William Shakespeare answered the question that may be on your mind: are some people just naturally people who really know?

Yes, there are individuals who just seem to be born with an extraordinary ability—like a math genius, a musical prodigy, a computer whiz kid or a chess grandmaster.

Shakespeare also wisely advised in *Twelfth Night*, "Be not afraid of greatness." We may not all be born a genius, but we're all born to be a person who really knows about something. Our mission, should we choose to accept it, is to figure out what that special knowledge is and then pass it on.

To be a disruptor, you cannot be doubtful. You have to believe that you're here for a purpose. You're here to realize your own revolution. Don't wait for the world to thrust greatness on you; thrust your greatness on the world. Someone's life is depending on it. I want you to really know that and take whatever action you can right now.

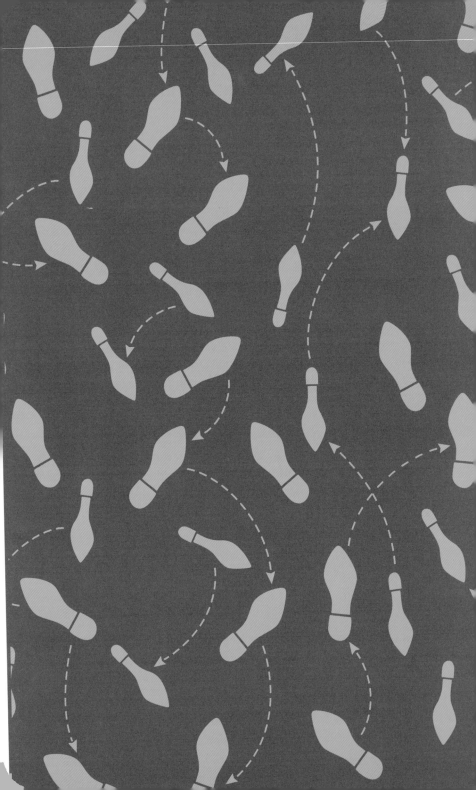

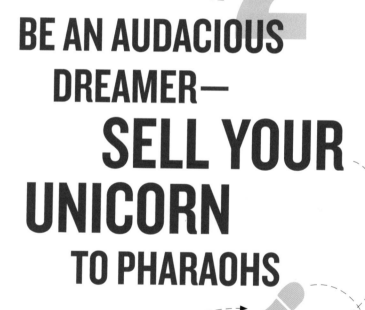

BE AN AUDACIOUS DREAMER—
SELL YOUR UNICORN
TO PHARAOHS

If you want to be a disruptor, you can be humble, but you can't be modest. You need a dream that's bigger than anything that gets in its way. Other people may call you crazy, monomaniacal or misguided. I call it audacious ambition. What are you out to achieve? Is it so big that others are too afraid to go after it? Tell everyone what you want to achieve with them and for them. Somebody will help you make it happen.

THIS SECRET IS for anyone who has the courage to pitch their dreams to people who have the power to make their dreams come true. It's for the people who are so hungry for success, they'll risk failure, over and over again.

I'm talking about all those times when you just go for it. You make the call. You earn the meeting with the people who actually make the decision. You step into your moment of truth. You put it all on the line. You know it's all up to you now. And you swing for the fences. It's the sweetest feeling in the world when you win. And it could just be the worst feeling in the world when you don't.

The first disruptor: Joseph

So, what's the magic formula? Well, let's turn to the first disruptor in the Bible, Joseph, because the technology changes but the themes are timeless. You may know Joseph's story, but not like I'm about to tell it.

Joseph was also the first Millennial. He was his father's favourite son. He believed he was destined for great things and his father loved him for it. But we all know that when you are the favourite you make enemies. Those enemies can be your brothers—and in fact, brothers can be the deadliest enemies.

Joseph was a man driven by audacious dreams, and he wanted to share his dreams with everyone he met. So he told his eleven brothers that the sun and the moon and the stars would bow down to him. That really annoyed them because they were just sheep herders trapped in their own mediocrity. They were scared of ambition. They were so angry at their brother's arrogance that they stripped him bare, threw him into a pit and sold him into slavery.

The sting

Joseph was sold to a wealthy Egyptian mogul called Potiphar. He immediately adapted to his new environment. He was so good at administering Potiphar's affairs that he gained Potiphar's total confidence. As a result, Potiphar made him head of his household and his trusted advisor.

Like all dreamers, Joseph was highly attractive to others because he radiated excitement and possibility. Potiphar's wife lusted after him, and Joseph became the first victim of sexual harassment. She made a move on him and he fled, leaving his coat in her hand. As a jilted would-be lover, she accused Joseph of attempted rape. Her word was worth more than his. He was found guilty and sentenced to prison with no hope of parole.

A second pit

Prison is a place where dreams go to die. It's also a place where people find their true character. Joseph may have been incarcerated, but he was still an audacious dreamer.

He gained the confidence of the prison warder and advised him on how to administer the facility more effectively. Soon he was the informal manager of the prison.

Joseph met two jailed servants: the pharaoh's baker and the pharaoh's cupbearer. Once again, because Joseph made it his business to talk to all the prisoners, both of them shared their dreams and fears with him.

Joseph gave them his interpretation. He told the baker that unfortunately he would be beheaded shortly. He told the cupbearer he would soon be back at his post. His only request of the cupbearer was that he mention Joseph to the pharaoh so he could get out of jail. Joseph was always looking for opportunity, no matter what his circumstances.

The opportunity

Two years later, the pharaoh was disturbed by what he saw. As a leader, he sensed a bubble coming. He had weird dreams in which he saw seven fat cows being eaten by seven thin cows. Then he saw seven healthy sheaves of wheat being eaten by seven diseased sheaves of wheat. He intuited that some kind of once-in-a-lifetime phenomenon was about to occur, but he couldn't pinpoint it.

He shared his bizarre visions with everyone, but no one could make sense of them. That's when the cupbearer remembered Joseph. He told the pharaoh about Joseph's ability to predict the future with uncanny accuracy.

The pharaoh called for Joseph. Joseph decoded his dream, predicting that wheat would grow abundantly over the next seven years. Then he predicted seven years of famine. He was so compelling that the pharaoh believed him. How did Joseph know? He didn't. He made the story up on the spot. He listened to his instincts. He made a bold call. He forecast the economic cycle. He spoke with imagination and conviction. Joseph ended up being right and that's why he became legendary. He could just as easily have been wrong.

The pitch

What happened next was the real reason for Joseph's success. He proposed a plan of action. He advised the pharaoh on how to profit from the coming commodity boom and busts. He proposed harvesting and storing the maximum amount of wheat possible in preparation for the seven years of famine. He gave the pharaoh a blueprint for setting up warehouses across Egypt.

The pharaoh was sold. He made Joseph his chief operating officer—the second most powerful person in the country. Joseph executed brilliantly. He made Egypt the wheat provider to the world at extremely inflated pricing. He built the pharaoh's status as a highly effective ruler and made him the richest person in the world.

Eventually, even Joseph's brothers, who had sold him into slavery, were forced to beg him for food. After taunting and teasing them for a while, Joseph forgave them wholeheartedly. And they lived happily ever after.

Joseph was one of the greatest audacious dreamers of all time. He followed his dream of power and prosperity. But Joseph's secret was his ability and willingness to share his dream. By doing so, he invited reciprocity—first with the servants, and then with the pharaoh himself. He then offered a clear plan of action.

Let's look at this story in a modern context.

The Joseph Pitch Code: How to pitch real-life unicorns to modern-day pharaohs

In today's world, we're all hunting modern-day pharaohs. They are the influencers, the mobilizers, the ones with the money and the power. Pharaohs can be male or female. They have become pharaohs because they either caused disruption or they survived it.

Because pharaohs have power, they face pharaoh-like challenges. For example, they are usually surrounded by yes-men. Like the old joke, pharaohs don't know if they are funny, because those around them get paid to laugh at their jokes. This means that pharaohs are looking for guts and authenticity. They want people with the courage to push back.

Pharaohs are also scared of losing their money and power. Deep down they know they are as vulnerable as the rest of us. They know that they need champions who can keep them on their thrones. They're looking for unicorns.

A unicorn is a horse with a horn. It's enchanting. It's mythical. It's also the disruptive idea or insight that could be worth millions. It's the thing that is most important to pharaohs. It's always the result of someone's dreams or vision. Joseph had it and so do you.

Here is the Joseph Pitch Code in nine simple steps. Evaluate yourself—in writing—against each one of the steps.

1. Have a big, bold, awe-inspiring, heart-stirring dream

Before you can make your dream come true, you need to have a dream. It sounds obvious but it isn't.

In my seminars, when I ask people about their dreams, the majority respond with a vague sense of what they would to like to achieve. It could be a house, a car, a vacation, a happy retirement, a promotion or winning the lottery. These are all nice things to have, but they are not dreams that will inspire the dreamer to engage in audacious actions to disrupt the status quo. In fact, most of these "dreams" are simply extensions of the status quo.

However, there's always an outlier in every group who gets it. They declare exactly what they want. One young guy at a financial services company pointed at the CEO and said, "I want *that* guy's job."

It's not always easy to hear

how amateurish you are,

but it's always thrilling

to see the improvements

in real time.

Another manager at a global retail chain that was introducing disruptive new technology said, "I want my store to be the one that people from around the world come to to see how it really should be done." A leader of a start-up health care company told me, "We want to build the best culture in the world so we attract the best people in the world." Another entrepreneur said, "I want to take my company from $20 million to $250 million in the next five years." When these audacious dreamers speak, the entire audience applauds. They don't see the declaration as arrogant; they see it as cool. They vicariously participate in the other person's dream and they are inspired to raise their sights. They start to believe that maybe they can make their dreams come true.

For example, from the age of seventeen, even though I stuttered badly, I dreamt of being a great communicator. I knew I loved to talk. But I didn't know there was an occupation called "professional speaking." After recovering from clinical depression in the early nineties, I wrote a book on my experience called *Lost and Found: My Journey to Hell and Back*. After its publication, I was approached by a professional speakers bureau to talk on the subject. I discovered a whole new way of making a lucrative living, one talk at a time.

My first professional speech was on July 24, 1993. It was good but not great. I stuttered throughout the presentation. My agent shared that the stuttering actually enhanced my delivery because it broadcast my authenticity. However, she told me that professionals don't stutter. They master their craft by rising above previous limitations. She introduced me to speaking coaches. They shared the fundamentals with me. I mastered my nerves and polished my delivery. My next speech was better, my next one better still. As a result, I've developed a lifelong appetite for coaching. It's not always easy to hear how amateurish you are, but it's always thrilling to see the improvements in real time.

Twenty-five years and two thousand speeches later, I've experienced a life of exploration and adventure. I'm still searching for the perfect delivery, but today I am as excited by the future as I was all those years ago. I may be in my fifties, but I'm still just a kid with a dream.

Technology and social media now offer me unprecedented access to the entire planet to share my dream. People living on different continents are inspired by my YouTube videos and my Twitter and LinkedIn posts. They watch my material and then approach me about talking to their teams. For example, that's how I won a marvellous assignment to speak in Amman, Jordan, in May 2017. The managing partner of the KPMG office there saw my video, liked my message and invited me to share it with two hundred leaders from the Middle East. That's the dream in action.

As I mentioned earlier, my dream for this book is to create a million disruptors who will transform their communities. That means I will sell at least half a million books and win at least 110 engagements in the next year. That would make me one of the top ten speakers in the world. It's going to happen. I see it first so others see it later.

What is your big, bold, awe-inspiring, heart-stirring dream? Imagine it coming true. What does this look like to you?

2. Declare your dream to everyone

Dreams are the raw material of disruption. Anyone can have a dream, but it takes the courage and boldness of a disrupter to put the dream out there to the world. A dream without an overt declaration is just idle thinking. It's the declaration of the dream that makes it audacious.

When Ryan Murphy was eight years old, he wrote a note to his parents. The handwritten note stated the little boy's big audacious dream. "I hope my swimming life continues and I become an Olympian when I grow up," he wrote. "I hope I will break records. I want to be the best swimmer in the world." The drawing attached to the note showed Ryan with a gold medal.[1]

Thirteen years later, the American swimmer picked up his first gold medal for winning the 100-metre backstroke at the 2016 Summer Olympics in Rio de Janeiro. Ryan won two more gold medals in Rio, one of them in the medley relay, which he swam with teammates Nathan Adrian, Cody Miller and Michael Phelps.

Ryan's story proves that a dream and determination can make you a world-beater. Ryan is a backstroker. I am a speaker. Tom Brady is a quarterback. Elon Musk is an inventor. What are you? Talk about it. The more you talk about your dream, the more real it becomes for you. The word is the seed of the deed. When you declare your dream out loud, it takes root in other people's minds.

I've also discovered that people who talk about their dreams are highly attractive to others. They exude vitality. They remind others that there are reasons to be excited. Their optimism is contagious. Their fire lights up others, especially in times of crisis or adversity. If people are energized by your presence, they are going to want a lot more of it.

On the television series *Shark Tank*, entrepreneurs pitch their ideas to celebrity investors. The show is in its eighth season and continues to achieve blockbuster ratings. Why? It is inspiring to watch people package and pitch their dreams to pharaohs. We smile at their ideals. We experience their nervousness. We empathize with their despair when they lose. We celebrate their wins.

It's time for you to participate in your own *Shark Tank*. How are you activating others into actualizing your big, bold, awe-inspiring, heart-stirring dream? What's your declaration of inspiration? When was the last time you refreshed it? When was the last time you risked sharing a big bet with others?

However, here's a warning: there are always detractors who will dismiss your dream, knock it down. They're skeptical, cynical and often indifferent or critical. They'll say no, not now, not ever. They will outnumber your champions. You'll hear, "that will never work" much more than you'll hear "I want to invest in your dream." The naysayers may even be right. Their naysaying may send you back to the drawing board, but only so that you can make your dream even more compelling.

Disruptors make their inner worlds part of their outer worlds by enabling others to see what they see. They describe their dreams in such a way that other people can see their dreams as clearly as they can. Think about an architect or a builder. They create computer-generated graphics and small-scale models of their creations that enable others to see their ideas for themselves. That's the difference between a dream and a hallucination—only you can see your hallucination.

Here is how Elon Musk and Tesla communicate their dream for Solar Roof in such a way that people want to install it:

Tesla's mission is to accelerate the world's transition to a sustainable energy future by creating products that are so compelling, there is no alternative. Solar energy has always been part of our master plan, and we recognized the need for a roof that is simultaneously affordable, durable, beautiful and integrated with battery storage.

Solar Roof complements a home's architecture while turning sunlight into electricity. With an integrated Powerwall,

Talking about your dream is like living the dream in advance.

energy collected during the day is stored and made available any time, effectively turning a home into a personal utility. Solar energy can be generated, stored and used day and night, providing uninterrupted power even if the grid goes down.[2]

The "master plan" was presented to the press on October 28, 2016. According to *Bloomberg Technology*, "The vision presented at Universal Studios in Los Angeles is the grand unification of Musk's clean-energy ambitions. The audience was able to step into a future powered entirely by Tesla: a house topped with sculpted Tuscan solar tiles, where night-time electricity is stored in two sleek wall-hung Powerwall batteries, and where a Model 3 prototype electric car sits parked out front within reach of the home's car charger."[3]

Tesla literally thrusts us into the dream. However, we can all provide people with a taste of the dream by offering samples of our offering—whether it's a service or a product. I produce short videos that give people a taste of the dream. Hollywood produces trailers of movies. What are you doing? Remember: every interaction with you provides people with a taste of what the actual end-experience will feel like.

Talking about your dream is like living the dream in advance. When you express it well, you'll find that other people want to hear more about it. They invite you to share it because they want to come on board.

There were probably people who laughed at young Ryan Murphy's note or Elon Musk's master plan. At the same time, there were people who immediately became champions. Who's laughing now?

The advertising for Johnnie Walker Scotch whisky says, "Keep on walking." I say, "Keep on talking." Keep on pitching. The more you tell others, the more you understand yourself, the better you become at sharing your dream, the greater the chances you'll find someone who believes you and believes in your dream. Partners will materialize all around you.

Modern-day Joseph would be sharing his dream online. He would be broadcasting his dream on multiple platforms to hundreds of like-minded disruptors. He would be accessing online funding such as Kickstarter and leveraging the heck out of his LinkedIn network.

3. Help other people interpret their dreams in a way that inspires them into action

Joseph deciphered the pharaoh's dream for him. It began as a montage of disturbing images in the pharaoh's mind. Through Joseph, it became a blueprint for global grain domination and unimaginable wealth accumulation. Joseph transformed the pharaoh from a worried chief executive to a leader with total faith in the future. He knew that his dream depended on executing the pharaoh's dream.

We're all agents of other people's success. The best disruptors enable everyone around them to become disruptors. They magnify other people's perception of what's possible. They help them make sense of things that don't make sense. Sometimes all it takes is the ability to listen with an open mind. It's a skill guaranteed to take your success to a whole new level. Joseph listened well. He didn't dismiss the dream or back away from the immensity of it.

Whenever I'm in the presence of pharaohs, I repeat back to them what they've told me. But I add my own spin and speculation about the implications of their intentions. I leverage my knowledge and my instincts. When I do it well, I hear the best phrase that a client can ever say to me, "Exactly, that's what I'm talking about!" After that, I know we're on the path to execution.

Are you a champion of other people's dreams? Do they share their hopes and aspirations with you because they know you will find a way to help them make their dreams come true? How can you become known as someone who helps others achieve their biggest goals?

4. Recharge your power in the pit

In 2004–2005, Martha Stewart served five months in federal prison for obstructing an investigation into her sale of ImClone stock. Instead of sinking into despair, Stewart used her time to continue to build her dream of a lifestyle empire. Even though she was literally behind bars, she kept the Martha Stewart brand alive and well.

Stewart put a plan into action. Finding that prison food was not acceptable (often well beyond the expiration date, she tells us), she found a way to make jam out of the crabapples from the trees in the prison yard. She worked on the outline of a book that was published shortly after her release, *The Martha Rules*, where she laid out her ten rules for achieving success in business. Stewart also helped build the dreams of her fellow female inmates by offering business advice.

In the introduction to *The Martha Rules*, Stewart writes, "There, amidst a thousand or so women, were hundreds of young, middle-aged, and older women who had dreams of starting a business when they were released. Many of them came to me to express their passion, their hopes, and their ideas."[4]

Despite what some regarded as a mighty fall, the Martha Stewart brand did not suffer. Stewart's book became a *New York Times* best-seller, and, at the end of her sentence, the stock price of her company was higher than when she entered prison. There is even a character in the Netflix women's prison series *Orange Is the New Black* based on Martha Stewart.

Martha Stewart clearly fell into a pit. Like Joseph, at some point she had to decide, "am I going to rot away in here, or continue to be an audacious dreamer?" We all know the answer. Today, at the age of seventy-six, she is as relevant and popular as ever.

A pit can be a hole in the ground. It also can be a mindset of misery. Either way, it's a place that tests our resolve and resilience. It's also unavoidable for disruptors. We get thrown into pits by our detractors, our environment, our problems or our own emotions. You have to be willing to spend time in dark, uncomfortable, lowly places.

However, pits are there to stop uncommitted people from carrying on. Pits are tests of our resolve and passion for the dream. That's where we need to double down on our commitment and ingenuity. That's where we need to look up so we can see the sun, the moon and the stars. Participate in your own rescue. Someone or something is coming for you if you keep looking for them. And remember: a specific individual may forget you, but destiny does not.

Two men look out through the same bars:
One sees the mud, and one the stars.
FREDERICK LANGBRIDGE

5. Protect your integrity

On every challenging assignment, there will be moments when you are tempted to give up. You feel momentarily overwhelmed by your circumstances. You question yourself and your ability to carry on. Those moments increase in direct proportion to the scale of your vision. Don't dilute your vision. Hold fast, hold strong. Make it bigger, not weaker. Develop a reputation for tough-minded reliability. Trust is the ultimate resource. Trust in yourself and others will trust in you.

You are your word. Your word is your reputation. Your reputation is your ticket to the pharaoh—especially your reputation as someone who reliably delivers results.

Integrity also means protecting yourself against distraction. Disruptors don't allow their focus to fade. They're single-minded in their pursuit of their dream. They know their intensity is their secret sauce. It makes their pitch authentic. Without it, nothing can happen. When it's gone, it's time to go home.

I hear a lot of people saying "work hard, play hard." You may not be able to do both at the same time. All the disruptors that I know avoid the kind of play that weakens their herculean capacity for work. Maybe the better expression is "work hard or play hard."

6. Model the future

The best way to predict the future is to create it. Lay out your plan with confidence and conviction. Provide a framework for moving forward. Detail the schedule of next steps. Show how actionable your vision is. Walk your pharaohs through the process. Spell out in detail how the dream will become reality.

Present your vision in a way that that moves your pharaohs at the deepest level. Talk with a conviction that defies resistance. Translate the moving images in your mind into pieces and things and signs that your pharaohs can see, hear or touch. Be a time machine: transport pharaohs into the future through the power of your ideas connecting with theirs.

Walt Disney Company popularized the word "Imagineer." Today, the Oxford Dictionary defines an imagineer as "a person who devises and implements a new or highly imaginative concept or technology." We're all imagineers. Joseph imagineered a brand new supply chain system. I'm imagineering the creation of one million disruptors. Elon Musk is imagineering the world's transition to sustainable energy. What are you imagineering?

7. Speak truth to power

I work with hundreds of sales and service people who need to engage with powerful, wealthy, well-known people for a living. They go stupid in the presence of power, wealth and fame. They

Make every conversation

a masterpiece.

lose their composure. They are intimidated and overawed. They feel weak and puny. Instead, they should feel the opposite. In that moment of engagement, all the power is with them. They are the ones who have the insights that pharaohs need. They are the domain experts who have the answers to the pharaoh's questions.

When you're pitching to pharaohs, the pressure is going to be on. Your dream is at stake. But you need to process the pressure as a stimulant, not as a constrictor. Remember: you've earned the right to be there or you wouldn't be there. Pharaohs are under huge pressure themselves. They're pulling for you to help them. They're looking for people they can trust to give them the goods.

I'm always in front of C-level leaders who are counting on me to help them achieve audacious ambitions. In fact, every leader with whom I work is out to achieve record-breaking results. That's the game—to do things that no one else has ever done. That's the kind of conversation you need to have. Talk straight. Tell it like it is. But also tell it like will be.

Make every conversation a masterpiece. Deliver a high ROT—Return On Time. Thrill the pharaoh with your perspective, your knowledge, your insights, and, most importantly, your understanding of how you can enhance their power. Pharaohs are scared of the bubble; they are scared of being mortal. Feed their ego intelligently. Look them in the eyes. Don't be intimidated.

Hey, it takes courage. It takes character. It takes brilliance. But if you cannot turn fear into fuel, you'll be stuck at the gates of paradise.

8. Have a passion for the grind

The African dung beetle is a model of stamina and ingenuity. It makes a living feeding off the poop of omnivores and herbivores, which is rich in nutrients and moisture. It is highly skilled in sniffing out fresh poop. It rolls a chunk of poop into a ball and pushes it all the way to its nest, which could be hundreds of feet away.

The dung beetle buries the dung in the earth and then goes back for more. In one night, it can bury up to 250 times its own weight in dung. It performs a remarkable role as both garbage collector and soil fertilizer.

But here's why I love the African dung beetle: it navigates by the moon and stars while it pushes its ball of poop to its nest. It's living proof that you can be inspired and guided by the heavens above you while you deal with the crap in front of you.

The dream is the spark. But the dream alone doesn't enchant the pharaoh. You need the ability to execute at scale. The business of business is excruciatingly tiresome. It's the attention to every detail. It's the process that details every milestone in granular detail. It's the ability to go fifteen rounds of raising money and then come back swinging for more. It's stamina at a Michael Phelps Olympian level. It's the discipline to do it right every time.

That's how you take the pharaoh with you across the finish line. It takes sweat to be mythical.

9. Forgive your detractors—the degrees of separation are shrinking

There's an old story about an angry young man and the Buddha. The young man did everything he could to get the Buddha to raise his voice. He insulted him, called him names. Finally the Buddha asked, "Tell me, if you buy a gift for someone, and that person does not take it, to whom does the gift belong?"

The man answered, "It would belong to me, because I bought the gift."

The Buddha smiled and said, "That is correct. And it is exactly the same with your anger. If you become angry with me and I do not get insulted, then the anger falls back on you. You are then

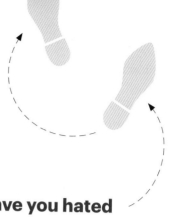

How often have you hated

someone and then found

yourself becoming that person?

Forgive your detractors

because you have to work with

them again. Keep your friends

close, keep your enemies closer.

the only one who becomes unhappy, not me. All you have done is hurt yourself."

Anger works in the opposite way to the way you want it to. It erodes your well-being. It corrupts your happiness. It narrows your bandwidth and hijacks your focus. It gets in the way of your clarity. It robs you of your empathy. It also leaps into your mind at the most inopportune moments. Anger also spills into hate. Hate is a toxic emotion that taints whatever it touches. It's the opposite of empathy and creativity.

How often have you hated someone and then found yourself becoming that person?

Forgive your detractors because you have to work with them again. Keep your friends close, keep your enemies closer. If you want to travel far, travel light. Just know that no one, except the sociopaths, does things just to hurt you. They did what they thought was right at the time. Unicorns have scars. Their horns didn't just grow over night. They're a result of insult after setback after mistake after failed promise after wrong turn. There are too few pharaohs to make anyone your permanent enemy.

Our world is hyper-connected. That pharaoh you insulted in your previous job may end up as your new boss. These shrinking degrees of separation are not your imagination. It used to be six. According to Facebook research, the new number is now set at 3.57.[5]

> **Be kind, for everyone you meet is fighting a battle you know nothing about.**
> **WENDY MASS, THE CANDYMAKERS**

Final thought: The dream economy

We are living in the dream economy. All the technology and the money is out there to make your dream come true. If you declare your dream, others will come to help you build it. Keep pitching your dreams to people who have the power to make your dreams come true.

Every champion I coach is a vocal dreamer. They may be loud or they may be soft. They may be extrovert or introvert. But they all are impassioned about their dream because it's bigger than they are. It helps them transcend their limitations because it's an expression of who they can become.

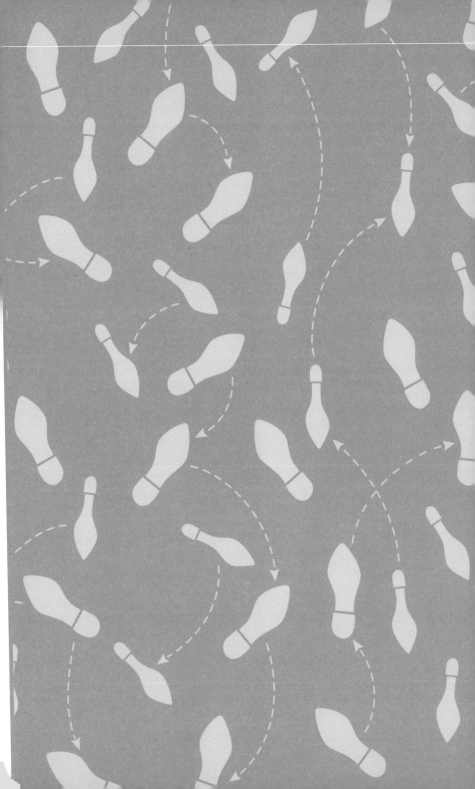

3

BE
SIMULTANEOUSLY
ANALYTICAL
ᴬᴺᴰCREATIVE

Disruption demands that left and right brain fire together. Your intuition may alert you to the opportunity, but it's your intellect that builds your business case. There may be a gap in the market, but is there a market in the gap? There may be hundreds of ways to do something, but which one way is the best way? You may have a hunch, but do you also have proof that your way is the right way?

AT THE END of 2007, I received a call from Ken Allen. At the time, Allen was the regional CEO for DHL, the global express logistics company, in Eastern Europe, the Middle East and Africa. He had just been made CEO of DHL in the United States. Unlike in the rest of the world, where DHL was the leader, it was a distant third in the US market, behind UPS and FedEx. Its network had been cobbled together through a series of acquisitions and had never gained any cohesion or operating synergies. In the United States, DHL was being massacred by its rivals, with total losses approaching $3 billion.

Allen quickly made the decision to pull DHL from the US domestic express logistics business. However, because of America's global significance, DHL needed to retain a foothold in the United States to service the international trade that was its forte. Allen applied his granular understanding of the business to strategically prune local operations and shed almost ten thousand staff. He then pivoted by positioning DHL US as a specialist in international shipping. Allen used DHL's presence in over 220 countries to brand it as "the most international company in the world." He introduced an internal training program to enable every single employee to become a "Certified International Specialist" and master the fundamentals of international shipping, which they could share with their customers and each other.

Allen had the vision and the courage to invest over $100 million in the world's biggest-ever employee engagement program. He made the "Certified International Specialist" distinction a unique competitive advantage for DHL throughout its global network. The program not only ensured that every employee did their job effectively, but it also became a powerful cultural phenomenon that brought the organization together "as one."

Within a year of taking on the US assignment, Allen was appointed global CEO. Eight years later, DHL Express is one of the most profitable growth companies in the world, with bottom-line profits well over the $1 billion mark. Allen is one of those great disruptors, able to be both analytical and creative. His years of experience enable him to see the patterns formed by the realities. He is someone who really, really knows the business. But it's his creativity and courage that enable him to turn crises and disruptions into winning strategies.

Over the past ten years, I have worked extensively with Ken Allen as a strategic coach. I've seen how he has been able to cascade his unorthodox methods throughout the organization. From creating global "DHL's got talent" competitions that enable employees to realize their dreams of being an entertainer on the world stage, to being the express logistics company for the Rolling Stones, Allen seizes every opportunity to pump up the volume. He's an accountant by training but he has the heart of a crooner. He breaks into song at every employee meeting. The organization's signature song is "Ain't No Mountain High Enough." It epitomizes DHL's commitment to being "insanely customer centric."

Greatness usually comes from a place of pain

It always begins with a negative. Something is missing. Something isn't right. Something isn't working. Something is annoying, frustrating, painful or just plain mediocre.

You see the problem. You feel the pain—whether it's yours or someone else's. It grips you and refuses to let go. You know the solution is out there somewhere. So you go looking for it. It becomes so important that you invest time and the energy into solving the problem. You study it closer. You talk to more people. You make it a personal priority. But still the answer eludes you.

Then you have your "aha!" moment. You could be in the shower, the car, the gym or the cinema. But you get it. You understand your next steps with exhilarating clarity. You're infused with the energy and excitement that comes with a big idea or a neat solution. In your mind's eye, you can see the prize and it pulls you toward it.

You share it with your family, friends, colleagues and customers. Their perspective enriches yours. You go further. You invest more time, energy and even money. You define your way forward in greater detail. You communicate your vision in a way that motivates others to support you. The stars align. You reach your first milestone. You make the sale. You win the assignment. You launch the product. You introduce your service. You begin your company.

Then you encounter one setback after another. Things don't go the way they should. You lose your momentum. So you try a different path. You formulate a different strategy. You recalibrate your approach. You find new partners and champions that expand your offering.

Bingo. You hit paydirt. You earn new customers. You grow your reputation. You generate the resources and infrastructure to build scale. You enter the high-performance zone. You pick up speed. You shift into overdrive. It's a beautiful thing. Until it's not.

Someone or something overtakes you. They become more attractive than you. They offer much more than you do. They make you look instantly dull or dated. So you feel the negative once more and go back to the beginning all over again. Repeat. Repeat. Repeat.

The disruption cycle begins with status quo. Then it becomes "dissatis-quo" as people encounter problems that are not currently being solved. Then the first disruptors emerge. Then they build their first supporters. Then they achieve critical mass. Then they achieve mass acceptance. And then it begins again.

Dancing with disruption means you need to see the problem in the first place. You need to see it before others see it. You need to understand the patterns and where they lead. You need to discern the minutiae that signal the bigger issues. Everything starts small. No one sees it until the first person does. It hides in plain sight. Then you need to do something. Nothing happens until someone takes action that persuades others to take action. Then it becomes obvious. This is the rite of passage for disruptors.

Disruptors get up close and personal with their chosen mission. They also step back in order to see the whole picture. They study the tracks their prey have left, but they understand the life their prey leads. They are part of the hunt and they appreciate all the elements that determine its success. They zoom in all the way to the minutiae and then zoom out to the macro view.

When you listen to a disruptor, you can hear their left (analytical) brain harmonizing with their right (creative) brain. You can

Analytics is the

science of disruption.

Creativity is the art.

hear their knowledge informing their imagination. That's why it's called an "in-sight." They see the idea or the notion inside their heads, and then they express it to others. At first, others may not see it because it may never have been expressed this way before. Disruption must appeal to more people than it alienates in order for it to become a disruption. So disruptors put the pieces together in a mesmerizing mosaic that captures others' imagination.

Analytics is the science of disruption. Creativity is the art. Disruptors toggle back and forth between the two. They know what they don't know. And they hire the people who know what they don't know.

The aha moment manifests itself long after it begins its incubation. Its seed is an acute interest in the problem that was originally identified. Then its growth depends on one's commitment to bringing it to life. For example, this book was seeded when I began searching for a topic to which I could dedicate the next year of my life. I need a "hot issue" that I can turn into a new program because new programs are my lifeblood.

Throughout the 2016 US elections, we heard about disruption, pivoting, overthrowing, revolutionizing, polarization, anger, frustration and rebooting. Violent, dramatic change is the order of the day in every bailiwick. Stability and calm don't live anywhere anymore. At best, they're tourists who come for very short stays.

Simultaneously, we're seeing a huge need for inner peace and well-being to neutralize the chaos outside. We're seeing robust growth in activities and industries focused on meditation, vitality, self-development, individual growth, community contribution, personal authenticity and soul journeys. A poster boy for this trend is Christopher Knight, iconized in the recent best-seller *The Stranger in the Woods*, who survived as a hermit in the woods of Maine for twenty-seven years without seeing another human being. We all have a part of us that wants to run away. But the vast majority of us are deeply connected to our fellow citizens. We love to engage each other. We can handle the turbulence most of the time, but we all have our tolerance threshold for chaos.

One of my aha moments was sparked by a request to deliver a keynote talk on how to achieve corporate goals by managing change and disruption. The client was single-minded in his commitment to making his target. But he was dismissive of the toll that the work was taking on his people. It simply wasn't a priority for him. He believed it was a price that everyone had to pay. His comment to me was that people needed to "cowboy up" and deal with their circumstances.

I knew there was a better way, because many of my clients are successfully pursuing the parallel tracks of simultaneously maximizing productivity and positivity. So I considered the concept of not just dealing with disruption but actually dancing with it. I developed a message of finding the joy in the disruption while you demonstrate grace and gusto in leading the way. That talk was the kernel of this book. It's the most important thing I have ever done because I'm doing it now and I'm doing it for you.

You've got to be willing to live with the pain of living in the gap between the situation you see and the situation you see it can become. It's the pain of frustration that comes from being able to see the possibilities that others cannot even imagine. You understand the patterns and where they lead. You discern the minutiae that signal the bigger issues. Somehow you know that the solution is out there somewhere. So you go looking for it. It becomes so important that you invest the time and the energy to solve it. You study it closer. You talk to more people. You make it a personal priority. The difference between a disruptor and someone who is just smart is that the disruptor does something about it. Growth of an idea depends on one's commitment to bringing it to life.

> You see things; and you say "Why?" But I dream things
> that never were; and I say "Why not?"
> **GEORGE BERNARD SHAW, BACK TO METHUSELAH**

The Adidas aha moment

It began with Kanye West leaping through the electronic flames at the Billboard Music Awards in May 2015. He was wearing a pair of white Adidas UltraBoost shoes that had never before been worn in public. Within the next few hours, there was a sales frenzy. Every single store that stocked UltraBoost shoes cleared out the shoe.

Until then, Adidas had been slipping. It had recently fallen behind Under Armour to become the number three sports brand in the United States. But Adidas, together with West, had created a moment. West's fiery UltraBoost debut turned Adidas's Boost technology into a cultural touchstone.

According to *Co.Design*, "By fall 2016, Adidas had overtaken Under Armour. The company's North American revenue soared by 30% from 2015 to 2016, with sales of UltraBoosts leaping 98%." The success reflects a strategy that "relies on celebrities as much as athletes." Market-research firm NPD Group has found that only a quarter of Americans buy sneakers for their intended athletic use. So Adidas has been "turning to cultural influencers as partners, dropping new shoe styles with increasing speed." Music impresario Pharrell Williams's "blocky, Lego-esque NMD line... sold almost a half-million units online and in stores on a single day on March 2016... these kinds of collaborations—along with Adidas's own in house efforts—represent a bold departure for the company, which is now treating shoes as fast fashion: stylish, responsive to trends, and engineered to hit the market quickly."[1]

Adidas sparked its renaissance when it was in its place of pain. Its sales and share price had dropped sharply throughout 2013 and 2014. It had also lost its number two position as an athletic brand to Under Armour. The share recovery since then reflects the market's intense passion for Adidas fashion. The shares appreciated from $35 in December 2014 to $115 in August 2017. By contrast, Under Armour's share price had plummeted from $68 in December 2014 to $18 in August 2017.

Today's wake-up call

Before we continue, let me ask you this: What has your aha moment been? Have you even had one? Did you take it seriously? What did you do with it? Has it led to anything material? Or is it just gathering moss in your neocortex?

You may be an accountant or an artist, a scientist or a salesperson, a bureaucrat or a builder, but if you're not creating and sharing ideas that excite you, you're probably just complaining.

If you're not promoting your ideas with passion, you're probably boring. And if you're not challenging the status quo, you're probably living someone else's dream or executing someone else's agenda.

How's that for a wake-up call? My wake-up call comes every time I lose an engagement that I fully expected to win. I find out which competitor won it. I review their message and their material. Then I reinvent my own. I constantly evaluate my offering against the myriad players on my space. I'm often blown away by my competition's creativity. I could be crushed by it. Instead I use it to crush it.

Even when I'm not shaken by an unexpected loss, I give myself a wake-up call every day because if I don't, something else will. I'm on it right now, writing these words. Every day, I have to outrun the people who are trying to overtake me. I also have to catch up with the people who are far ahead. Like the cheetah, Africa's fastest predator (which can reach speeds of up to fifty miles per hour), I miss my prey half the time. But like the cheetah, I'll never be found under a tree deciding that I'll give up and become a vegetarian.

Fly social, not solo

An idea created in the mind is just daydreaming. Unless you take action, it doesn't mean anything to anyone. You can't win if you keep it to yourself. Winning comes from creating in public, manifesting the idea in the marketplace. It's only worth what others are willing to pay in terms of time, money or buzz.

Next you need wingmen or wingwomen to complement your capacity. So you share it with your family, friends, colleagues and customers. Their perspective enriches yours. You go further. You invest more time, energy and even money. You define your way forward in greater detail.

Never before have we had so much technology that enables collaboration and innovation. Yet many people are reticent to share. They don't want to give up control. They're not prepared to do the extra work of curating multiple points of view. They don't trust others with their ideas. They'd rather complain. (Just check out most of the posts on Twitter.) But if you're a disruptor, you reach out to anyone who can help you as often and as effectively as you can.

That's when the stars start to align, you reach your first milestones, you make the sales, you win the assignments, you launch the products, you escalate your success.

Who can you reach out to to accelerate your disruptive innovations?

We're all left-and-right-brain creatures

One of the great myths that I want to debunk is the notion that people are either exclusively right brain, the domain of creativity, or left brain, the analytical and rational domain. The truth is that we're a combination of both and we can toggle effortlessly back and forth.

According to *Fast Company*, "While the right side of the brain remembers the gist of an experience or the big picture, the left side of the brain recalls the details. Complex cognitive functions require the regions of the brain to work in an integrated fashion, shifting between divergent and convergent thinking to combine new information with old and even forgotten knowledge. People may feel more comfortable looking at concepts over minutiae, and vice versa, but the more easily you shift between both sides, the more complex a creative a thinker you can be."[2]

Divergent thinking refers to the problem-solving strategy characterized by proposing a multiplicity of possible solutions to determine the one that works best. Convergent thinking is a problem-solving technique that brings together different ideas from different participants or fields to determine the single best solution to a problem.[3]

Fast Company also reported the results of a 2008 study by Robert Epstein, a psychology researcher, founder and director emeritus of the Cambridge Center for Behavioral Studies, and senior research psychologist at the American Institute for Behavioral Research and Technology. The study demonstrated that

> by developing four core areas—capturing new ideas, engaging in challenging tasks, broadening knowledge, and interacting with stimulating people and places—people can enhance their brain's ability to innovate. Seventy-four city employees in Orange County, California, participated in creativity training consisting of exercises that focused on these four proficiencies. Eight months after the training, the employees increased their rate of new idea generation by 55%, brought in more than $600,000 in new revenue, and saved about $3.5 million through innovative cost reductions. So while some people seem to be less adept than others at firing up both burners, making them appear more left-brained than right-brained, most brain scientists agree–and this is what's exciting–that the ability to shift rapidly between divergent and convergent thinking, which is the key to innovation, can be sharpened and improved.[4]

Unleash the glory in the ordinary: Purposely lose the ability to take anything for granted.

Writing about David Hockney's retrospective exhibition at the Tate Britain in London, Ian Brown observed in the *Globe and Mail*, "Genius may be 2 percent inspiration and 98 percent perspiration,

> **If you aspire to pre-eminence, ordinary is always an opening to extraordinary.**

as both Edison and Einstein said, but it is 100 percent confidence as well. You can feel Hockney's daring in every room of the show."[5]

David Hockney has been called one of the most popular artists of all time. His genius is his ability to express the glory in the ordinary. Review his work online. He depicts everyday situations and objects as fragments of a dream that enchant and inspire us in equal measure. At the age of eighty, he continues to experiment with new approaches, including drawing on an iPad. As Brown writes, "Watching his iPad drawings come together on the screen as he drew them, you still shake your head at his sheer skill, at his unerring eye."[6]

Hockney is one of the most gifted individuals of all time. But so are you in your own way. You may not be awarded a major exhibition at the world's most prestigious galleries, but you can earn your equivalent honour with your key stakeholders. Getting an audience with you right now is my Tate moment. So is every seminar with every client. A favourable comment from just one advocate of mine is thrilling kudos. I've purposely lost the ability to take anything for granted.

If you aspire to pre-eminence, ordinary is always an opening to extraordinary. If you view your surroundings through the lens of a disruptor, you delight in the details because they are the building blocks for breakthroughs. You're willing to invest the time because you know inspiration isn't always instant. Sometimes it's a composite of many images, facts or numbers that coalesce over time.

Frustration is the genesis, not the nemesis

Continuous effort—not strength or intelligence—is the key to unlocking our potential.
WINSTON CHURCHILL

James Dyson, the founder and CEO of Dyson, the highly innovative manufacturer of vacuum cleaners, hair dryers, fans and heaters, wrote in the *Globe and Mail*,

> Failure is just part of the process. It took me 15 years and 5,127 attempts to develop the first bagless cyclonic vacuum. I won't lie—it was frustrating, aggravating—but it was also invigorating, exciting. What matters about failure is that you learn from it... Perhaps the biggest thing that holds inventors back might be our impatience... It's important to teach people... that if you fail once, you're one step closer to success... Because it's failure that drives invention forward.[7]

There's a reason why the lubricant known as the "can with a thousand uses" is called WD-40. In 1953, chemist Norm Larsen made thirty-nine attempts to create a line of rust-prevention solvents and degreasers for use in the aerospace industry before he found the one that worked.

Frustration is defined as the feeling of being upset or annoyed, especially because of the inability to change or achieve something.

Disruptors know that they have to make friends with frustration in the short term. They have to make frustration their genesis, not their nemesis. Frustration is the birthplace of creativity if you can master it. It's the enemy if you cannot.

When I came to Canada in January 2001, I partnered with the Environics Research Group to create a new kind of motivational program that blended powerful social values with impactful actions. I could clearly demonstrate how idealism, individualism and commitment to one's community could be translated into everyday actions for success. What's more, I could do it in a way that resonated deeply with the front line. All the motivational programs to that point focused on mental principles or cosmetic techniques. At the turn of the millennium, I saw the need for a social values–based methodology that would enable people to thrive in a brave new world.

For the first six months of our joint venture, I literally went door to door talking to anyone who would listen to me. Many Canadian prospects told me that they were interested but they didn't want to be the "guinea pigs." They told me to return to them when I could prove the effectiveness of our formula. American prospects were more direct—either they declined my approaches or they told me they had never heard of Environics or Mike Lipkin and were therefore not interested.

Then, in July 2001, I persuaded the largest professional service company in the world, Deloitte, to hire me as a keynote speaker at a marquee conference for their senior managers. The presentation was a huge success and I leveraged it to merchandize my services across both sides of the border. People started to listen to my pitch. By the beginning of September 2001, I had built a pipeline of lucrative engagements across the continent. Then 9/11 happened. The motivational speaking industry collapsed. No one wanted to get on a plane, let alone listen to a "motivational speaker." It was ironic—this was the moment that I believed I was designed for. Yet no one was in a mood to listen. Instead of participating in formal sessions for hundreds of people, I spoke to everyone I could reach, one person at a time.

Over the next six months, I also refined my material to reflect a radically different reality. All of a sudden, people cared about what was happening in a remote part of the planet. They discovered their exposure and vulnerability to the world's horrors. But they also discovered their interdependence and mutual connectedness. Most of all, they discovered their capacity to carry on.

In that context, my message was prescient. By mid-2002, the market had recovered and my business caught fire. Over the next fifteen years, I would deliver almost two thousand talks, publish six best-selling books and become one of the leading speakers in North America.

However, in my world, just like yours, disruption is a daily phenomenon. This book is how I'm dancing with it. How are you doing it?

Do you consider yourself creative?

Just as I may not think of myself as intensely analytical, you may not think of yourself as intensely creative. But creativity simply means doing something differently to improve the outcome—the greater the difference, the more disruptive the outcome.

In a global benchmark study, Adobe Data conducted research on five thousand adults in the United States, the United Kingdom, Germany, France and Japan to uncover how creativity is perceived and valued. The results revealed that in the United States, only 52 percent of respondents described themselves as creative (and that was the highest of all the regions!). Curiously, seven out of ten people in the same group also believed that creativity was important to the economy.[8]

But I believe that 100 percent of us should perceive ourselves as creative. Creative thinking is an innate ability in each of us. Being a disruptor demands it. The challenge is to truly understand your role and play it the best way you can today. Then reinvent the way you play it tomorrow.

Based on Environics/Lipkin research and interactions with over a million people over the past seventeen years, I've identified five categories of creator/disruptor. I guarantee that you are exceptionally talented at one of these five kinds of interdependent creativity. Where do you see yourself?

- **An inventor**—You literally invent the new product or service. You are a pioneer, explorer and experimenter. You march to the sound of your own drum. You're always way out in front, so others have to stretch to follow you. You are a one-person, early-solution system. You're continually in search of the new and unprecedented.

- **An enhancer**—You take an existing product or service to the next level. You are a fast follower. You are the one who enables the inventor to bring their creations to market. You sharpen the saw, polish the edges and iron out the bugs. You unlock potential by translating the inventor's vision into reality. You ask, "what if" and "how about?" and "can we?" Without you, the revolution remains stalled at the gate.

- **A connector**—You are able to align teams and communities around the new product or service to accelerate their socialization. You listen. You talk. You share. Your middle name is Social. You love to hang with people and it shows. You introduce people to things and things to people. Enhancers reach out to you to make their products and services go viral. Your favourite question is, "Have you heard about . . . ?"

Creative thinking is

an innate ability in each of us.

Being a disruptor demands it.

The challenge is to truly

understand your role and

play it the best way you

can today. Then reinvent the way

you play it tomorrow.

- **A protector**—You work within the rules to maximize the financial and compliance aspects of the business. You keep people on the straight and narrow so they can spread their wings and fly. You make sure it's always kosher but you never forget that you're an enabler of success. You do whatever you can to give people the green light, but you're always ensuring they don't go too far.
- **An administrator**—You sustain the existence of the new product or service by being great at the grind. You are relentless and tireless. You have a passion for the particulars. Nothing escapes your attention and nothing goes awry on your watch. When you're on the team, your teammates can rest easy. You stand guard at the door to prevent Murphy's Law from making mischief.

Understand your bailiwick and then operate within it. As the great Dirty Harry said, "A man's got to know his limitations." Or, as I say, play from your sweet spot. Once you understand your suite of strengths, exercise them as far and as hard as you can. You'll be surprised at how far they take you. I am an enhancer and connector. Everything I do, including this book, performs those two roles.

In the best companies, the culture makes room for everyone. These companies know that when you've got too many adults in the room there's not much creativity. They also know that you have to have at least one adult in the room to keep an eye on the details.

Regardless of your role in an organization, being a disruptor involves creativity.
What role do you play?
Where must you ramp up your impact?
How can you be creative in enhancing your contribution?

Applying data creatively: It has to be "Now what?" not "So what?"

It's no coincidence that the five most valuable companies in the world are the giants who trade in data, the oil of the digital era: Alphabet (Google), Amazon, Apple, Facebook and Microsoft. Data are to this century what oil was to the last one: a driver of growth and change. From subway trains to jet engines, all sorts of machines are becoming sources of data. Through the IoT—Internet of Things—everything is being linked to everything.

For example, even an industrial behemoth like General Electric is reinventing itself as an analytics company. It has developed a software platform called Predix to help its customers control their machinery. Predix is also a data collection system: it pools data from devices it is connected to, mixes these with other data, and then trains algorithms that can help improve the operations of a power plant, determine when to maintain a jet engine before it breaks down, and the like.

The greater one's access to data and mastery at managing it, the more ingenious one becomes at finding ways to lead disruption. The data has been democratized but turning it into growth fuel takes both commitment and creativity.

Jan Kestle is president of Environics Analytics, Canada's leading provider of data-driven marketing solutions. She has been a thought leader in the marketing information industry for over forty years. In a wide-ranging interview with her, she shared with me six key insights on mastering data:

1. Understand the problems you are trying to solve.
2. Speak in a way that everyone can understand without sacrificing technical detail that is important to them.
3. Put yourself in others' shoes and ask, "How can I give them

what they need to succeed?" When using data, think about your stakeholders and how they need to consume the data.

4. Data is an enabler. It is only useful if it translates into action. It has to be "Now what?" not "So what?" Data has to help your stakeholders make more money. For example:

   • How can I help the people in my call centre know what to offer next to customers based on what's going on in the conversation?

   • Can I differentiate between customers who come into my stores to simply compare prices and those who genuinely want to buy?

5. Be an activist who seeks to reshape the way the functions engage each other and the results that are achieved. One of the biggest barriers to results is the lack of sharing of data by people across the enterprise. Break down the silos and encourage people to share their data in ways that build their brands and businesses.

6. Test all kinds of approaches. You can learn from that, and then tweak. You can fail faster so you can succeed faster.

One of the fascinating ways in which Kestle and her Environics Analytics (EA) team applied data to achieve literally life-saving results was with the London, Ontario, Fire Department (LFD), through its "Fighting Fires with Marketing Analytics" campaign. Using customer segmentation and data analytics expertise provided by EA, the LFD's 2013 campaign identified those who caused the most fires, determined their lifestyles and values, and then developed a targeted marketing campaign featuring differentiated messages designed to reduce risky behaviours. In 2012, residential fires in London dropped by 22 percent, saving lives, reducing injuries and averting potentially millions of dollars in property damage—and the approach is now being adopted by fire departments across Ontario. Fire Chief John Kobarda of the LFD said, "Using analytics to understand the demographics behind who is having fires, and where similar groups of people reside, enabled us to use a targeted and tailored approach to the first two lines of defence: education and prevention."[9]

What disruptors know for sure

Life is about duality—left and right, up and down, light and shadow, north and south, expenses and income, far and close, yes and no. Everything has its opposite, but not its contradiction. Left doesn't contradict right, just like debit doesn't contradict credit. It complements it. It validates it. It completes it. Disruptors dance with this kind duality.

This is what the disruptor knows for sure:

- **Comfort and creativity are allergic to each other.** Safe space is really the most dangerous space because nothing new and exciting lives there. You go there to rest and recover, not to create breakthroughs.

- **Disruptors aren't afraid of creating in public.** The paradox of creating in public is that taking the risk of failing publicly protects you against the risk of failing privately. Regret is far more painful than imagined "loss of face" from actually trying something new that doesn't work. In an age that celebrates the quest for innovation, your stature may actually grow with every false start.

- **Losing is neglecting the opportunities to make an impact.** Lost opportunities lead to more lost opportunities. Losing can become a habit. Winning isn't just about winning. You can do everything right and still get it wrong. Winning means being worthy of your gifts by giving all you can as often as you can. Creativity is a muscle that needs the regular exercise of both thinking and acting.

- **You don't have to be perfect to act.** You don't even have to be good. Acting is how you become good. The right thing to do is to do it right now. Then course-correct as you go along.
- **Creativity is finite and infinite.** A great idea stands alone but creativity is constantly being renewed. Creative people don't run out of ideas, so they're not afraid of people copying their ideas. They know that great ideas are shared ideas.

Beyoncé: The art of surprise

At midnight on December 12, 2013, Beyoncé changed the music business forever. She launched her eponymous fifth album without warning by posting a single word—"Surprise!"—and a videoclip to her Instagram account. She had secretly loaded her entire album, consisting of fourteen songs and seventeen videos, onto iTunes. That was all it took. Beyoncé used her 53 million Facebook followers to bypass traditional media. Twitter reported 1.2 million tweets in the first twelve hours. The album sold over 800,000 copies in the first three days, making it iTunes's fastest selling album worldwide.

The next album released by Beyoncé was *Lemonade*. Once again, she surprised the world. Unveiled during an April 23, 2016, HBO special that had been advertised as a world premier event (with no further details), the twelve-song *Lemonade* collection was streamed 115 million times in the first six days alone.

Beyoncé understood the new realities, and opportunities, of the music industry. It wasn't just the shockingly abrupt nature of the launches that wowed the world, it was the combination of music and video.

Beyoncé explained her concept of a visual album in a press release: "I see music. It's more than just what I hear. When I'm connected to something, I immediately see a visual or a series of images that are tied to a feeling or an emotion, a memory from my childhood, thoughts about life, my dreams or my fantasies. And they're all connected to the music."[10]

Like no one else, Beyoncé visualizes the music and how it can be connected directly to her fans. That's the power of seeing things that others haven't while you surprise the world with your vision. I'm trying to coach people on how to dance with disruption. How are you planning to surprise others?

Disruptors don't let missteps get in the way. They push through the frustrations and the doubts. It's about urgency but it's also about patience.

Final thought: Get ready to deep-dive then soar

My goal for this chapter was to cause a ripple that inspires you to put it out there. What idea do you have that gives you wings? What will motivate you to create in public? What will enable you to fly above the fear of failure? How will you be simultaneously both analytical and creative?

Getting your left brain and right brain working together means a deep dive into the detail followed by a soaring scan of the ways to turn the detail into opportunity. Then you need to do something. Nothing happens until you take action that persuades others to take action.

Disruptors don't let missteps get in the way. They push through the frustrations and the doubts. It's about urgency but it's also about patience. The best thing about the future is that no one has been there yet. We're all making it up as we go along. Disruptors are just getting there faster because they're simply thinking more and doing more.

Lipkin's eight steps to being simultaneously analytical and creative:
1. Think about what you can create that excites you—within your strengths.
2. Carve out the time to develop your thoughts and share them with others.
3. Record your ideas as they come to you. Keep a journal— virtual or physical.

4. Choose your best idea and promote it to the people it will help the most.
5. Develop it by publishing it.
6. Champion it with knowledge and passion. Enroll others. Help them take ownership of it.
7. Refresh it, reinvent it or repurpose it when required.
8. Let it go if it isn't working and begin again.

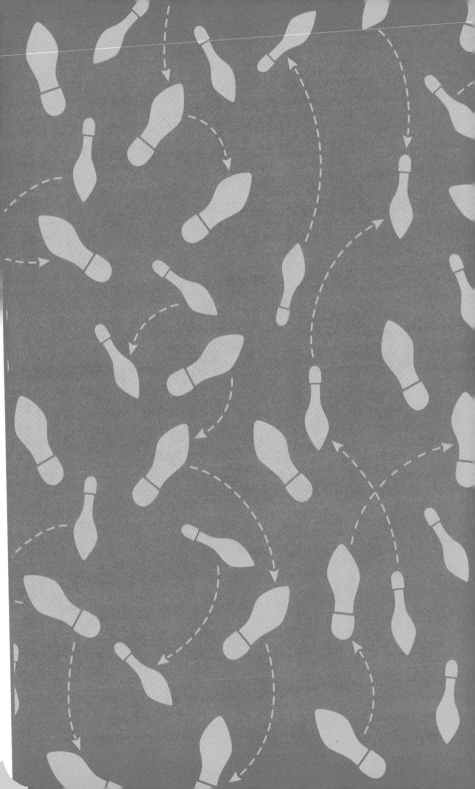

4
BE
PROLIFIC

Disruptors try a lot more things than disruptees.

They fail fast and they fail forward.

The more you lose, the more you win. Version

1.0 is always imperfect. You will hear

the word "no" hundreds of times more

than you'll hear the word "yes." The

best way to get ready is to do things before

you're ready. The best you can do is to make

it as perfect as you can the first time

and then make it more perfect. The

philosophy of being prolific is do more so you

learn more so you can achieve more.

MARK WAHLBERG HAS starred in over forty movies. In real life he has been a criminal, a musician, a model, an actor, a producer, a businessman and a restaurateur. He is renowned for his commitment to personal health and reinvention. He has also created an iconic status for himself as the ultimate everyday American hero who will save the day when no one else can. Now in his late forties, he is still known as "the Body" because of his athletic physique and his habit of displaying it onscreen as often as he can.

Wahlberg also displays another trait of disruptors: he hustles. Disruptors do a lot of things all the time. But they're not frenetic. They pack a huge amount into their days but they are also in control of what they do. They are in charge of their own life and choose their activities according to their priorities. One thing for sure is that disruptors understand the fleeting nature of every opportunity. They prepare for the future by solving what's now. They live and work large because they have trained themselves to be that way.

As Jamie Millar recently wrote, "Wahlberg does a lot of things at the same time, none of them by half. To some, he's almost more businessman than he is actor, although he doesn't completely agree. 'Acting is my primary business,' he says. 'But I'm 110% committed to both.'"[1]

Highly productive people leave us breathless with what they accomplish. Director, producer and screenwriter Francis Ford Coppola is known for legendary films such as *The Godfather* and *Apocalypse Now*. But Coppola doesn't limit himself to films. He founded American Zoetrope, an independent film studio in San Francisco; created the literary magazine *Zoetrope: All-Story*; and operates a booming winery and a hotel business. Plus he's a tuba player.

Condoleezza Rice is another prolific champion. For most, she is best known for her work as Secretary of State and National Security Advisor with the George W. Bush administration, her expertise in Russian politics and history, and her distinguished academic career as a professor at Stanford University. When she was younger, Rice was a dancer and competitive figure skater, and was on her way to becoming a classical pianist. She speaks Russian, French, Spanish and German, as well as "football." Because of her knowledge and passion for America's favourite pastime, in 2015 she was appointed to the select committee that picks the top college football teams in the United States. In short, Rice can discuss the Middle East or a middle linebacker with equal aplomb.

Wahlberg, Coppola and Rice are poster people for being prolific on an epic scale. But we can all pursue our own brand of prolific. So I will write a book every two years, deliver one hundred speeches a year, coach twelve high performers every month, mentor multiple millennials on their way up, manage a multi-million-dollar financial portfolio, and invest in early-stage start-ups. It sounds exhausting but it's really exhilarating. If you commit to the philosophy of prolific, you magically find a way to do it all.

Being prolific is not for the faint of heart or the short of breath. It's a commitment to a tempo that would intimidate lesser mortals.

> **Being prolific is not**
>
> **for the faint of heart**
>
> **or the short of breath.**

But it's also not workaholism. It's an integration of work and play that rejuvenates one's spirit and stretches one's capacity. The English educator and philosopher L. P. Jacks expressed it beautifully when he wrote, "A master in the art of living draws no sharp distinction between his work and his play; his labor and his leisure; his mind and his body; his education and his recreation. He hardly knows which is which. He simply pursues his vision of excellence at whatever he is doing, and leaves others to decide whether he is working or playing. To himself he always appears to be doing both."[2]

James Patterson—The Henry Ford of writing

James Patterson is one of the world's most prolific authors. In 2016, he published sixteen books and in 2017 over twenty. On any given week, Patterson has at least one book on the *New York Times* bestseller list and sometimes even two. He has created more enduring fictional characters than any other novelist writing today, with his Alex Cross, Michael Bennett, Women's Murder Club, Private, NYPD Red, Daniel X, Maximum Ride and Middle School series. According to the biography on his website, Patterson had sold over 350 million books worldwide (as of January 2016) and holds the Guinness World Record for the most #1 *New York Times* best-sellers. In addition to writing thrillers, he writes children's, middle-grade and young adult fiction and is the first author to have #1 titles simultaneously on the *New York Times* adult and children's best-seller lists.[3]

According to Todd Purdum in *Vanity Fair*, Patterson is "the Henry Ford of books." He "writes seven days a week, 365 days a year. Writer's block is never a problem. If he ever gets bored or stymied with one active project, there are a dozen others to turn to at any one time."[4]

Patterson himself has said, "I'm not a writer's writer. I'm not a craftsman. I could be, and that would be a one-book-a-year operation."

There may be a trade-off between absolute perfection and practical excellence. Disruptors are willing to make it. They know that experience is the greatest accelerator of success. But they don't try to up the ante on their own. As an author, Patterson is unique in his partnership with co-authors. According to the *New York Times Magazine*, "To maintain his frenetic pace of production, Patterson now uses co-authors for nearly all of his books. He is part executive producer, part head writer, setting out the vision for each book or series and then ensuring that his writers stay the course."[5]

Patterson is an extreme role model for the philosophy of prolific. But he is also an extreme example of how to achieve unprecedented success through an intense work ethic combined with a disruptive penchant for creative collaboration.

Four principles for being prolific

1. Live by the law of abundance

Creating in large numbers is the ultimate law of nature—build in abundance in anticipation of attrition. When you apply this concept to thinking and innovating, it means knowing that the vast majority of new ideas do not make it through infancy. Many will perish without making an impact. Only the mightiest are memorable. You have to endure the ideas that don't succeed so you can execute the ones that do. By definition, when you do a lot of things and learn from each one, some of them are going to work.

The law of abundance protects you from becoming attached to a single idea or outcome. If you only have a few tricks, your success is going to be short-lived even if the tricks work. But if you're imagineering new tricks all the time, you always know that you're about to produce bigger and better ones that will. You vaccinate yourself against the vulnerability that comes with limited options.

When my clients think of themselves as being trapped or jammed into a "box," they're always going to be unhappy and ineffective. The moment we identify a range of options together, their mood lifts and so does their productivity. There are always more ways out of every problem and more ways into every opportunity. We just have to find them.

I write, I post blogs or videos, I speak, I read, I learn. I keep doing these things to take advantage of the law of abundance. When I post a message that resonates with my audience, I gain the potential to reach thousands more at no extra effort to me. And the more people I empower, the greater the chance that some of them will hire me to coach their teams. I follow the philosophy of the sperm cell: about two hundred million are ejaculated. Only one needs to find the egg.

Disruptors create their

own lottery and massively

stack the odds in their favour.

They interpret their

results in a way that

empowers them to win.

2. Make your own luck

The truth is that luck is a matter of chance. That means it is distributed equally across everyone. We have studied millions of people in many countries. The difference between lucky and unlucky is the bias toward action or non-action. It's not more luck that makes the difference, it's the return that one generates on luck—ROL (Return On Luck). The more prolific you are, the luckier you become.

Stephen Graham, a legendary Canadian entrepreneur, calls himself "the luckiest person I know." He is one of the disruptors with whom I work who consider themselves to be lucky. Yet they have never won the lottery. They don't even play the lottery. They're not subject to "lottery thinking." If the odds of winning the prize are literally one in 13.9 million (as with the Ontario Lotto 649 for June 28, 2017), it's lunacy to even play it unless you're intentionally engaging in a fantasy.

Disruptors create their own lottery and massively stack the odds in their favour. They interpret their results in a way that empowers them to win. Every thought triggers an emotion. Every emotion triggers an action. Every action triggers a result. Every result triggers a momentum—negative or positive. Some people call this luck. I call it "earned success." LUCK really means Labouring Under Correct Knowledge.

Disruptors expect to win because they do whatever it takes to win. They have zero sense of entitlement but they believe in commercial karma. They are all citizens of ROME—Return On Massive Effort. They accept the ad hoc bad breaks and the wrong calls because they know it will all play out favourably in the end. The system is their friend. The force is with them. That's why they never give up. The prize is always waiting for them at the end. And if it's not, it's not the end.

When I hear disruptors explaining their success by saying, "I was just lucky," I know it's not false modesty. They believe they are blessed. As human beings, we have a choice as to how we view our lives: we can believe every event is random or we can believe every event happens for a preordained reason. If we believe the former, then it's impossible to create our own luck. If we believe the latter, then we can preordain it through the right actions. That's what I believe.

Every time we win, we earn a deposit in our Belief and Confidence account. Winning reaffirms us. It charges us up. It ratifies and vindicates us. It's the wind beneath our wings. That's why they call it a streak. It looks like we're moving fast and effortlessly in a desirable direction.

Winning also has an enormous appeal to the people we seek to influence. We radiate a level of certainty that is contagious. We have what other people want even if it is just in that moment. Our challenge is to sustain that delicious feeling of unstoppability when we encounter the inevitable defeat. No champion ever goes undefeated. At some point, the problem is temporarily bigger than we are. The competitor is temporarily better. The prospect is temporarily blinded to our charms. That's when we have to remember that losing is part of winning.

While we will all lose more than we win, it's the wins that define us as winners. You're reading this because I made it across the finish line. That's all that matters. You can't see the false starts and the wrong turns because they don't matter. Cheers!

3. Practice mindful repetition

We have all been at the receiving end of a sales pitch that's been delivered so many times it's robotic and clichéd. Or we've been served by someone who is just going through the motions. We've also all experienced the quiet desperation of being that way ourselves. We hear ourselves saying, "here we go again" or "same old, same old" or "I'm tired of this."

This kind of repetition is like suicide by instalment. It will erode you into extinction. Mindful repetition means performing each task like you're doing it for the first time every time. It means being wowed, not wearied, by the experience.

Tim Hortons promises us that their treats are "Always Fresh"— not sometimes fresh, or never stale. Can you make the same promise about yourself? The irony is that we have to practise being always fresh, otherwise we will go stale. It demands being intentionally inspired every time we step on stage.

Céline Dion has been called the most profitable music act in Las Vegas since Elvis Presley. Her show has been seen by over two million people. I saw her just after her one thousandth performance in October 2016. She radiated an authentic joy that captivated the sold-out crowd. She told us that all she wanted to do was sing to us that evening. She told us that we completed her life and she was thrilled that we had given her the privilege of performing for us. I believed her, as did everyone else in the house. How could one not believe her when she sang with such verve and joie de vivre? It didn't matter that she had done it a thousand times before. What mattered was that night.

Céline Dion was paid almost $500,000 for her time that night. She earned every penny. But let me ask you: would your performance improve if you were paid $500,000 per meeting? Practice acting like that's true and see the difference.

"Practice" is the most important word in the vocabulary of disruptors. Practice is defined by the Random House Dictionary as "repeated performance or systematic exercise for the purpose of acquiring skill or proficiency; condition arrived at by experience or exercise; the action or process of performing or doing something." The key words are: repeated, systematic exercise, purpose, condition, action, process, doing. "Practice" is an active verb but it's also a state of being. We refer to a professional's "practice." That is literally where the professional works, but it's also something that they have built through their repeated actions over time.

It's easier to act your way into a way of thinking than think your way into a way of acting. Read that statement again. *It's easier to act your way into a way of thinking than think your way into a way of acting.* We learn by doing. We get ready to do something by doing it before we're ready. That's how we become ready. On the other hand, just sitting and thinking by yourself in a dark room may prepare you for nothing more than more inertia.

When we discipline our practice and practise our discipline, we increase our capacity to achieve remarkable results. We develop an operating rhythm that builds our momentum. In his book *The Way of the Fight,* the renowned Canadian mixed martial artist Georges St-Pierre says, "I have a belief that all human greatness is founded on routine, that truly great human behaviour is impossible without this central part of your life being set up and governed by routine. You don't get better on the days when you feel like going. You get better on the days when you don't want to go, but you go anyway."

4. Hunt for breakthroughs

One of my favourite activities in Africa was to leave behind the trappings of city life and go to a game park. As a speaker, I would often participate in corporate retreats held in these remarkable locations. On rare occasions, we would witness a pride of lions catching and feasting on their prey. I was always struck by how violent it was. While the lions executed a practice refined over many hunts, there was no instant "killer blow." It would take lion after lion to leap onto the prey and try to pull it down. The buffalo or the zebra or the wildebeest would fight back with horns and hooves. Often it would escape. And even when the lions were successful, it was a battle of attrition. The prey would be worn down by multiple assaults until it succumbed to the fatal bite. It was bloody and exhausting for hunter and prey alike.

The hunt for breakthroughs creates its own breakthroughs.

Every time the lions set out to hunt, they expected a titanic battle with their prey. Even though they are masters of their craft, they don't expect it to get any easier. They also see every hunt as the only one that matters. And so do I.

It's not the pursuit of happiness, it's the happiness of the pursuit. The hunt for breakthroughs creates its own breakthroughs. Whatever we search for is what we tend to find. Our senses are programmed to locate what is hidden to others.

We've all witnessed the whirling dervish—the person in the gym talking on a cell phone in a raised voice and frantically waving their arms, or the individual in the restaurant balancing a tablet in one hand, a glass of wine in the other, constantly taking calls, totally indifferent to their surroundings or the person in front of them. That's frenetic, not prolific. The difference is awareness, focus and mastery.

If you're hunting for breakthroughs, you're acutely aware of the opportunities around you. You are willing to experiment with new approaches and lines of attack. If you succeed, you systematically repeat your activities in order to become proficient at them. If you don't, you try a new approach and begin again. You'll discover that even the "failures" yield immense dividends. Every time I've pursued a big prize, I've been able to repurpose my investment of time, whether I won the prize or not.

The five greatest blocks to being prolific

You've seen it happen many times. At the beginning of a project or enterprise, people are highly engaged. They're ready to rumble. They're on fire with possibility. They're up to trying anything. Then they pass some kind of threshold and lose their mojo. They stall. The odds are that they stumbled against one or more of these five blocks to being prolific.

1. Lack of love for the work

Total engagement is a prerequisite for doing more without burning out.

There is a direct correlation between being a disruptor and being engaged with your work. The heart goes first and the head follows.

In the United States, 70 percent of employees are not engaged with their work, according to Gallup's 2017 *State of the American Workplace* report.[6] Gallup finds that less than half of US employees (41 percent) strongly agree that they know what makes their company's brand different from that of competitors; therefore, they can't effectively communicate it to customers.

Disruptors, on the other hand, either find work that they love or find something they love about the work. They're passionate about their purpose. Without passion, being prolific is impossible. It's just too much pain without concomitant reward.

Just like me, you've engaged in projects that took all you had and then some. There were moments when you wanted to capitulate to frustration and fatigue. But you stayed the course because the highs were worth the lows. You believed in the mission. You cared about the people you served.

2. Lack of energy

There is no lazy person's how-to book on disruption. There is no guide that provides a formula for "having it all" by sitting around and doing nothing. Disruption requires sustained intensity. Stamina is a core ingredient of being prolific. This includes making a physical commitment to your own well-being. In the game of life, it's not about who is right. It's about who is left.

This doesn't mean you have to have the body or the endurance of a Mark Wahlberg. When you speak, you don't need to channel P. T. Barnum. Disruptors can be extremely effective without making a lot of noise. I have worked with disruptors who are quiet and understated. I have also worked with disruptors who are rabid self-promoters. All of them, however, get stronger as the game goes longer.

Unless you're a comic-book hero, there is no such thing as scaling tall buildings with a single leap. It's one step, one toehold, one risk, one drop of sweat at a time. You know it's going to be hard, but you make it look easy. You know you will ultimately prevail, but you're willing to push harder than anyone else along the way to ensure your success.

Inaction is also an action. If you don't try anything new, you will reap the penalties of inertia. You'll watch your competition carry away the spoils. You'll live your life with the pain of procrastination. You'll become one of those people who let their magic fade away while they blame the world for letting it happen. But that's not you, right? Congratulate yourself for having the energy just to read this book.

3. Lack of perspective

Frustration, despair and anger warp our view of the world. When we "lose it," we lose our capacity to see things as they really are. We inflame our response out of all proportion to the moment. And we often ruin our relationships with others forever.

Lack of perspective can seriously derail efforts to be prolific. One needs to place specific circumstances in the context of the overall goal. There is an empowering reason for everything. You need to find it in order to take the next action with gusto and zest. Today's no is simply a stepping stone to tomorrow's yes.

For example, if you make $10,000 on a deal and you have to make ten calls to close the deal because the first nine people turn you down, then each "no" is worth $1,000 to you. So you haven't received nine rejections, you've received $9,000 that can be cashed as soon as you receive the lone "yes." In that light, disruptors feel lucky to hear the word, "no." It means they're on their way to multiple "yeses."

At a recent event in North Toronto, a young Indo-Canadian woman shared with me that she believed in reincarnation. Then she told me she must have been exceptional in previous lives to come back as a Canadian. I laughed, but she wasn't joking. Every morning she wakes up believing that she's won the lottery just by being born in Canada. That's why she is enabled by an enormous sense of well-being and gratitude. Makes you think, doesn't it?

> **If you ever** hear the language of blame coming out of your mouth, it is a sure sign that you're a disruptee on your way to becoming even more miserable.

4. Intolerance of failure

In our research at Environics/Lipkin, people tell us their biggest fear is the fear of failure. It's the fear of looking bad, losing status, falling short, getting fired, disappointing oneself or disappointing others. It's an internal story that kills one's drive and willingness to dare.

One of the biggest mistakes that losers make is that they think losing is failure. They confuse delay with defeat. They beat themselves up for results that may have been inevitable or unavoidable. They turn a setback into an indictment of their ability or personality. They feel the pain without perceiving the lessons that point to the solutions.

Prolific producers don't suffer from the rampant anxiety that stops others in their tracks. They have graduated from the most debilitating question in business today: "What happens if I fail?" They know that pain is often the raw material of extraordinary achievements. They tolerate the sting of unpleasant surprises because they know that kind of pain is both inevitable and indicative of future gains.

As noted in the *New York Times Magazine*, "Psychologically, we are steadily becoming more apprehensive than ever, with—according to the National Institute of Mental Health—18 percent of people experiencing actual anxiety disorders in any given year."[7]

An anxiety disorder is where fear about the future paralyzes you in the present. But you can't be paralyzed if you're out there trying new things. When you're in motion, you're moving somewhere—forward, backward or sideways. It doesn't matter. You're mobile. You're engaging your world on a range of contact points. You stand a chance of bumping into the right person or solution. As Dani Reiss, CEO of Canada Goose, says, "Lightning will not strike you if you don't go out."

Beth Comstock, the Vice Chair of General Electric, articulates the power of failure beautifully: "For most of us mere mortals, we're in continual failing mode. Sometimes the failures are big, sometimes they are small... It's a daily process, and it doesn't always feel great... When I fail, I know I'm on the ropes but still in the game, which is the only place I ever want to be. The small, daily grind of failing and learning is how we get better. And for some types of knowledge, it's the only way to get them."[8]

5. Desire for perfection

The desire for perfection is a doubled-edged sword. On the one hand, it is a powerful impetus for success. It fuels the drive to make things better and become the best. On the other hand, it slows you down. It restricts the number of iterations that go live in the marketplace. It robs you of the insights that users provide when they actually consume your products or services.

The truth is that perfect is a moving target. It's also a subjective interpretation. It can always be more perfect. Disruptors know that the goal is never "perfect." It's "perfect enough." Lorne Michaels, the legendary producer of *Saturday Night Live*, said it best: "The show doesn't go on because it's ready. It goes on because it's 11:30."

> **If you want to succeed, double your failure rate.**
> **THOMAS J. WATSON, SR., CHAIRMAN AND CEO OF IBM**

Being prolific in the marketplace: ZARA

Inditex is one of the world's largest fashion retailers, with eight brands and more than seven thousand stores in eighty-eight markets and twenty-nine online markets. The company's workforce exceeds 150,000 people. In its 2016 fiscal year, Inditex generated revenue of over US$25 billion.

Zara, Inditex's flagship store, has a clearly identified target market: value-conscious millennial and teen fashionistas who want to wear the trends as they happen. Zara makes the promise that when you visit one of its stores you will always be buying something nearly unique.[9]

With this strategy of being prolific in place, Zara has managed to buck all of the ugly trends in the retail market. The retailer doesn't have to stock a lot of clothes, and updates what's in stores regularly. Turnover of stock is extremely rapid. Its almost two thousand stores receive deliveries of new clothes twice a week. This "benefits the company in two ways: one, it doesn't have to resort to excess sales to rid itself of inventory, and two, it encourages consumers to shop with a sense of urgency—something that consumers don't have when it comes to shopping at a Banana Republic or J. Crew, when they have been conditioned to buy everything on sale."[10]

Zara's also incredibly swift at adapting, since it operates on a fast-fashion basis. This enables Zara to pivot immediately toward abrupt changes in fashion or weather patterns. When you combine the above with Zara's phenomenal operating supply chain and the way it manages its inventory so well, it is not hard to see the reasons behind the chain's success.

The *New York Times Magazine* has said that Zara has completely changed consumer behaviour, quoting Masoud Golsorkhi: "When you went to Gucci or Chanel in October, you knew the chances were good that clothes would still be there in February. With Zara,

You don't fall in love with your own brilliance, because it's only brilliant when your clients or customers embrace it.

you know that if you don't buy it, right then and there, within 11 days the entire stock will change. You buy it now or never. And because the prices are so low, you buy it now."[11]

Generating new ideas and value through social media: Mike Lipkin

My business model is a function of creating new material that is sent to my network of thirty thousand people around the world every four weeks. All I need is a handful of people to be in the market for that message. Maybe they were planning a conference, maybe they realized that they needed coaching, or maybe I just sparked a desire to excel. But every month, I know I'm going to hear the sweetest phrases in my vocabulary: "Your timing was perfect. Your message was exactly what we were looking for. We want to hire you."

I call this approach having a "consultant's mindset." It means you focus on how you can bring the best value to the people you're endeavouring to influence. You don't fall in love with your own brilliance, because it's only brilliant when your clients or customers embrace it. I can have my little victory when I say something that gets applause, but then I must keep going. It's time for the next idea.

The timing may not always be right for my next great idea, but it will always be right at some time. I can pitch the best content to the most appropriate client and still not make the sale. They just weren't in the market at that moment. But I can make exactly the same call the following month and achieve immediate success. The secret is to keep on creating content and making calls, both to the same people and to new ones.

How are you going to be prolific?

Fashions may change, but highly effective business models and mindsets stand the test of time. Zara is about instant adaptation to a rapidly changing environment. James Patterson is about churning out gripping stories that are seductively easy to read. Mark Wahlberg is about perpetual motion around an everyday hero ideal. Mike Lipkin is about creating new motivational programs every four weeks and promoting them at almost zero incremental cost through YouTube, LinkedIn and Twitter. What are you about?

How long are you taking to pivot and shift in response to market forces? Are you demonstrably ahead of the curve or are you sucking in someone else's fumes? How rapid is your metabolism?

How prolific is your output?

Are you evolving faster than your competition and the world around you? Or are you lagging? How do you know?

Final thought: Being prolific makes you ready for miracles, and being ready for miracles makes you prolific

It was a miraculous victory. With under ten minutes to play in the 2017 Super Bowl, the New England Patriots were down 28–12 against the Atlanta Falcons. According to ESPN, the odds of the Falcons winning the game were 99.6 percent. However, the odds are there to be defied by the champions. In the first Super Bowl that went to overtime, the Patriots staged the greatest comeback of all time, winning 34–28. In his post-game press conference, quarterback Tom Brady said:

When you do everything

that you can do and then

some, you plant the seeds for

miracles to happen. If you

play all the angles, something

will always reveal itself.

You go through the sequence of the plays and how many critical plays needed to be made. Coach [Bill Belichick] talks about situational football and there was so much of that that went on to score two, two-point plays like we did, down 16 points against a great football team. It was just a great team performance. I'm so proud to be a part of this team. We faced a lot of adversities over the course of the year and overcame them through a lot of mental toughness. It was a great way to culminate the season. We've got into this place before and not finished it off the way that we wanted. It took a kind of miraculous effort to do it. I'm just so happy that we were able to get it accomplished.

According to *USA Today*, the Patriots "practiced for this": "'We paid a serious price to get to this point,' Patriots receiver and special teams standout Matthew Slater said. 'We put in a lot of work. We're practicing in pads on Super Bowl week. We're squatting 80% of our maxes on Super Bowl week. I mean, we worked for this. Our bodies were ready. Our minds were ready, and we just kept believing in one another.'" Nobody panicked or got demoralized, Slater said. It was business as usual, even in the only overtime game in Super Bowl history.[12]

When you do everything that you can do and then some, you plant the seeds for miracles to happen. If you play all the angles, something will always reveal itself. The Patriots would not have made history if they weren't ready for it. And they wouldn't have prepared so intensely if they didn't expect to win in the first place. I put in the effort because I know the effort always pays off. Winning is always pretty; getting there isn't. Blood, sweat, guts and tears are the disruptor's favourite ingredients.

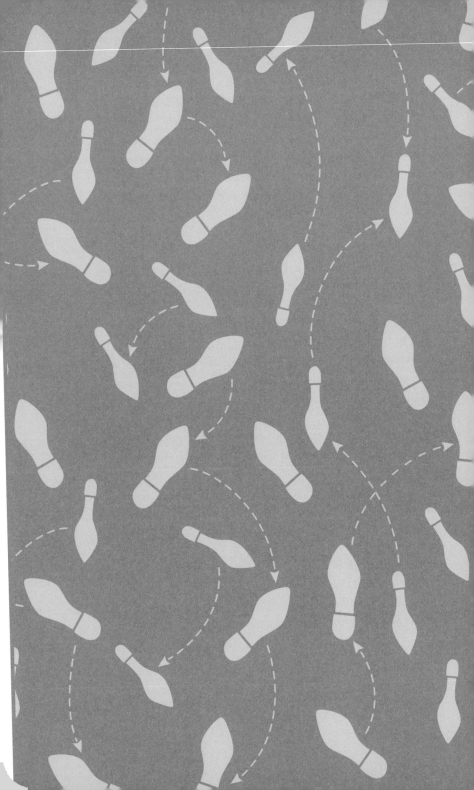

5

COMMUNICATE
LIKE
MAGIC

Words are packages of emotion that have

a physical impact. They inflict pleasure or pain.

They don't just describe things, they

define things. Our words become our world.

The way we communicate determines

the way we live. Communicating like

magic is a skill that can be learned

and mastered by anyone. It's the capacity

to transform people through information and

inspiration. The right words at the right

time are the moments that shape our lives.

WE'VE CHOSEN YOU. *You're amazing. Well done. Congratulations. Thank you so much. We really appreciate you. You nailed it. You vastly exceeded our expectations. You've made us look so good. We are delighted with your work. You're a true professional. You've won all our business. You've earned our total trust. You have brought a whole new dimension to our company. We admire everything about you. You conduct yourself like a champion. We would like to make you a firm offer. We look forward to partnering with you.*

These are not just phrases, they're physical injections of pleasure. As you read these words, dopamine (pleasure hormone), endorphins (mood enhancer hormone) and oxytocin (love hormone) started flowing through you. You're still on a high. You want to read further because there is more magic in store.

Words are packages of emotion that cause chemical changes in our bodies. They conjure up images that immediately transport us to places in our minds. If you say the right words, you attract others to you. If you say the wrong words, you repel them. I'm continually amazed by the power of words to switch people on, especially when they're delivered in a compelling way.

On the other hand, I'm constantly surprised by how much damage the wrong words can inflict on someone. The worst phrase

I ever want to hear from someone is, "I'm offended by your words." That means I've broken the connection. I've raised a wall between us. I've lost that person's trust, maybe forever. Elephants have got nothing on humans. It's humans that never forget.

Think about the word "magic." It has a thrill to it, right? It sparkles. It shimmers. It floats above the ordinary. It's fascinating. It means that something highly desirable is about to occur. It represents a new set of possibilities that weren't there before. We know it when we hear it. We're charmed by it. We're curious about it. We're excited by it.

Magic may sound like an exotic word for an accountant, engineer, doctor or lawyer to use. But they are exactly the kind of people who need to communicate like magic. They need to communicate their ideas and solutions in ways that captivate and motivate others to take action on their recommendations. It just takes a subtle shift in emphasis to make the difference, as you'll see shortly.

Of all the insights that I've shared with you so far in this book, this may be the most powerful: words don't just describe things, they define things. Our words become our world. The way we communicate determines the way we live. Nothing has any meaning except the meaning we give it through our words.

In the past twenty-four years, I have spoken to over a million people in forty-three countries. I have researched millions more. Less than 1 percent are intentional in their vocabulary. That means they consciously choose their words because they're mindful of the impact that their words have on others. That's why they reap disproportionate rewards. They understand the enormous power of mindful communication.

Mindful can also be spontaneous and authentic. Being deliberate doesn't mean being disingenuous. Like everything else in this book, it's a dance. It's understanding the right moves to make and then making them in rhythm with the music or whatever other sounds your environment is making. Your mind can toggle back and forth in real time between what you're actually saying and the way you need to say it. The one informs the other. The more you do it, the better you become.

Of course, communication is more than just words. But words flavour everything else we do. While words alone may not make magic, without the right words no magic occurs. If you say it, you can do it. But if you don't say it, it can never be done. Words are the seeds of deeds. Enrich your words and you'll enrich your life.

There may be times when silence is golden, but there are even more times where silence is crippling. Our greatest regrets are always around what we didn't say rather than what we did. In the absence of communication, people fill the void with speculation. Often their speculation is completely divorced from reality, but they act as though their thoughts are the truth. So when in doubt, say something. If you practise what I'm about to share with you, you'll always say it well.

I'm excited to share my composition "Communicating Like Magic" with you. It's taken me over fifty years to learn the ten elements that follow. While you may be familiar with some of the concepts, see them in the context of the whole. See yourself as a composer about to create your own personal symphony. Play through each element. Practise them as though your success depends on it, because it does.

1. Inspire yourself

Wherever you are right now is your entire life in miniature. Whatever you feel right now is entirely within your control. It's up to

> **Amateurs wait for inspiration. Professionals make their inspiration. They know that nothing happens until they're ready to make it happen.**

you to inspire yourself, irrespective of circumstances. It's easy to be inspired when you're in the presence of greatness. It's easy to be happy when you're surrounded by happiness. The secret is to find the inspiration inside yourself, especially when you're confronted with VUCA—Volatility, Uncertainty, Complexity and Ambiguity. When things are at their worst, it's time to play at your best. That's when everyone else is waiting for someone like you to lead them.

Amateurs wait for inspiration. Professionals make their inspiration. They know that nothing happens until they're ready to make it happen. So they constantly scan their environment for reasons to be upbeat, excited, enthusiastic, optimistic, grateful, appreciative or empowered.

I'm writing these words on a Saturday afternoon in May. I can see the blossoms outside my window. I can hear the coffee percolating. I feel the sharpness that comes from hours of sharpening my mental saw. I'm focusing on the success of this book and the huge impact it will have on thousands of people. I'm looking forward to my trip to the Middle East and Europe in the next two weeks. I'm proud of the work I'm doing.

How could you inspire yourself right now? Why could you be upbeat, excited, enthusiastic, optimistic, grateful, appreciative? What do you need to think about? What do you need to focus on? What do you need to listen to? Who do you need to watch? What do you need to read? Make it a habit.

I can tell you from experience that I have never delivered a poor presentation when I've been inspired. I have never offended anyone because I showed how happy I was to be with them. I have never regretted anything that I've done out of gratitude.

2. Be conscious of yourself, but don't be self-conscious

Be aware of how you're acting. Observe yourself from outside of your own head. Imagine you were watching yourself on someone else's iPhone. How would you appear?

At the same time, don't be so concerned about your optics that you're only thinking about yourself. If you try too hard to look good, you'll end up looking bad—or inconsequential at best. Focus on other people's experience of being with you. Be conscious of how you make them feel.

I have developed a technique called MCTV—Mental Circuit Television. I watch myself when I'm in front of others. I ask myself how I would feel if I were them. I challenge myself to make every conversation a masterpiece. I make sure that I'm not doing anything that would annoy or irritate others. I control my gestures. I make sure that I am rewarding them as richly as possible for their time and attention.

Think about all the times you have caught yourself being inattentive. You became aware that you were distracted. You saw the look in other people's eyes. You sensed their hurt or disappointment that you weren't paying attention to them. You felt regret after the meeting because you didn't bring more to it.

From this moment on, commit to being fully cognizant of how you're being when you're in front of others. Resolve to project the best version of yourself no matter what the circumstances. Uncensor yourself for the sake of others.

I know that this may be harder for the introverts reading these words. You may feel an involuntary reticence in public moments. Your natural shyness may constrict your willingness to act in a manner that inspires others. That's okay. But you need to get over it. I know it's easier said than done. But here's a huge aha: the disruptor's desire to disrupt is bigger than their fear of being rejected or embarrassed. How badly do you want to make a difference? How painful is it for you to sit on the sidelines instead of being on the field helping your team win? Remember why you need to communicate and you'll find the how.

While being too soft robs you of your voice, being too loud or extroverted can appear to others as being self-centred or egotistical. The golden rule is to be guided by the actions that will inspire others to be their best by spending more time with you.

3. Express your personal style

Your style is the distinctive manner in which you act or talk. It's your special look, feel, sound and, yes, smell. It's what differentiates you from everyone else. It's the signals you send to others that determine their reaction to you.

When we meet other people for the first time, we immediately brand them as potential friends or enemies. We feel a sense of

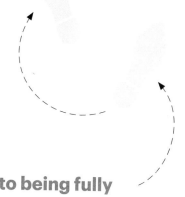

Commit to being fully

cognizant of how you're

being when you're in front

of others. Resolve to project the

best version of yourself no

matter what the circumstances.

Uncensor yourself

for the sake of others.

camaraderie or alienation. We experience instant comfort or discomfort. We decide whether they are like us or they're different. We relax with them or we tense up.

You can't please all the people that you want to please. But you can maximize your success by living the perception that you want other people to have of you. So what would you like other people to say about you? What do you want them to feel in your presence? What is the look, feel, sound and smell that is truly you? How can you project the right profile while you're being truly authentic?

When I ask people these questions, they struggle to respond. The questions are not difficult. It's just that most people haven't clearly considered them. Well, it's time to become your own publicist. It's time to champion yourself, because if you don't who will? In a world where the competition is so strong, every move matters.

This entire book is an expression of my personal style. I want people to perceive me as a uniquely inspirational, approachable, enjoyable, knowledgeable, energizing, reassuring strategic coach, advisor and motivator. I want people to feel empowered, confident and unstoppable in my presence. I want to look fit, fresh and fashionable. I want to project the image of someone who gets better as he gets older. In short, I want people to see me as an agent of their success and a model of what's possible.

Anyone who knows me, including my wife, who knows me best, will tell you that I live the descriptions that I have shared above. I don't have to work at being those things. I am those things when I'm being my best. My mission is to live that way every day.

Of course, there will be days when we fall short of our ideals. But even a mediocre day spent chasing our ideals is better than any other day just going through the motions.

Take care with your emails

How many emails do you send to business associates every day? What do your emails say about you? Do they express your personal style? Email may be the way that we communicate with others most frequently. Every communication counts. Check your grammar. Check your spelling. Check your formatting. Show how much you care about the recipient by showing the care you take in communicating with them.

Be careful about relying too much on tech tools like voice recognition software. When a computer decides what you mean, you could be in trouble. The other day I read an email that said, "I need an assistant that is efficient, cheerful and *reproductive* under pressure." You can't make this up!

Style beyond words

Marilyn Monroe once commented that all it took to conquer the world was the right pair of shoes. She had a point. The way you express personal style through what you wear is a core differentiator. People are influenced by what they see. If you are blind to your own style, those who follow you might not take you seriously.

Sartorial style clearly expresses your brand. Steve Jobs's outfit comprising New Balance running shoes, black turtleneck and Levi's was his signature. Mark Zuckerberg's T-shirts and hoodies are the same. Lady Gaga's and Madonna's outfits are strategically outrageous. Amal Clooney's cosmopolitan glamour redefines what it means for women to be powerful, brilliant and totally glamorous.

My style is classic, fitted and smart. I want to showcase my commitment to personal health and vitality through the clothes I wear. When I look smart, I feel smart.

What's your style?

It's your move

Physical movement and stance say a lot about you. Confidence has its own language. Disruptors move as though they own their domain. Their gestures radiate their passion or authority. Even something as simple as gait projects a message.

For example, if I were to observe you walking toward me, what would I think of you? Would I believe that you know where you're going? Would I believe that you're relaxed or tense? Would I want to talk to you or walk away from you? Do you look like you belong there? Or do you look like you're out of place?

We literally need to walk our talk so we can ensure consistency between our words and our movement.

4. Rehearse your spontaneity

If you have ever watched live theatre or an exceptional stand-up comedian, you have seen performers demonstrating rehearsed spontaneity. They are so well prepared that it appears as though they're responding from the heart and gut. They have invested so much effort that their delivery seems effortless.

They don't operate by rote. They are continually elevating their delivery. They have the confidence to improvise their material, confidence that comes from rigorous practice.

My definition of confidence is simply having done the thing before. The first time is always the most nerve-racking. Once you've done it, you know you can do it better the next time.

As Shakespeare wrote in *As You Like It*, "All the world's a stage, / And all the men and women merely players; / They have their exits and their entrances; / And one man in his time plays many parts." We're all actors playing our roles. We're all delivering value to the stakeholders in our lives. We need to keep improving our performances if we want to keep playing our parts.

No matter what your role, you are first and foremost a communicator. Your success is a function of the confidence you instill in others. The more spontaneous you seem to be, the more authentic you will appear to be. No one sees your preparation. They just see your performance. Make it great.

One of the most common findings in our research is that people struggle with feeling "inauthentic" when they take on new roles. They are caught between the justifiable need to "be themselves" and the necessity of acting like the person they need to become in the new role. By definition, anything is going to feel awkward in its early stages. That's not a reason to avoid it. It's a rite of passage. All the magic is outside our comfort zones.

According to Herminia Ibarra, an economist and professor at London Business School, "When we view authenticity as an unwavering sense of self, we will struggle to take on new challenges and bigger roles. The reality is that people learn—and change—who they are through experience... By trying out different leadership styles and behaviours, we grow more than we would through introspection alone. Experimenting with our identities allows us to find the right approach for ourselves and our organizations."[1]

From this moment on, intentionally "act the part" you've taken on. Recreate your style as you go. In the beginning, it won't be comfortable, but it may turn out to be right for you. You don't know what you don't know. All you know is what you've tried in the past. For all you know, the real you is still being formed—role by role, conversation by conversation. Whenever you say, "This just isn't me," you cut yourself off from further breakthroughs.

5. Connect at a visceral level

"Visceral" means deep, emotional and internal. It comes from the word "viscera," which means the internal organs of the body. So when you connect with someone at this level, you bypass the rational boundaries. You go straight to the heart and gut. You establish immediate trust and rapport. You become the agent of disruption or the antidote to disruption, depending on the role you're playing. You leverage techniques used by the best marketers and advertisers in the world.

In short, you apply seven core principles of connection—just as I have been doing throughout this book. If you even apply just one of these principles, you'll see an immediate impact:

1. You compliment your prospects authentically. You declare your admiration for others in terms of who they are or what they've achieved. No one ever gets enough recognition or appreciation. We all want to feel liked, loved and respected. If you don't mean it, don't say it. But if you go looking for a reason to praise someone, you'll always find one.

2. You demonstrate how similar you are to others. You use their words. You demonstrate that you share their values. You even mirror the way they speak—fast or slow, soft or loud. This is not manipulation. It's putting others immediately at ease so they don't allow their discomfort to interfere with their perception of you.

3. You create language that evokes a unique image in your prospect's mind—like "dancing with disruption." Those two

"When the music changes so does the dance."

concepts are not normally associated with each other, so they are moving, memorable and aligned strongly with you.

4. You use words that suggest valuable inside knowledge and the competitive edge. Words like secret, principle, formula, recipe, ingredient, chemistry, method, strategy, flight plan, blueprint. We are all listening for signs of mastery and know-how. We form instant opinions of people that can last the entire duration of your relationship. If someone perceives you as an authority from the first moment, it's easier to reinforce it with your subsequent actions.

5. You package your information in terms and graphics that are fresh and familiar, bold and safe, daring and conservative. You find the balance between taking the leap and providing a safety net. In the face of disruption, people are looking for both elements all the time. In the financial world, it's called hedging. We're all looking for ways to maximize our return and minimize our risk in every aspect of our lives.

6. You position yourself as a coach and catalyst of others' success. You talk about yourself as someone who is totally committed to helping other people win. Then you provide proof. You want to be an ally to all and an enemy to none.

7. You detect others' patterns of focus and dance with them accordingly. There is an old African proverb that states, "When the music changes so does the dance."

   For example, there are people who immediately default to "no" or "can't" or "impossible" or "too difficult." You indicate that you understand how hard they believe the action is and you identify with their doubt or fear. Then you reassure them you'll do whatever it takes to make it easy, successful or achievable.

   Or someone indicates that they are in a hurry or short of patience. You speed up your delivery and get to the finish line faster. The opposite also applies—if you are with someone who likes to take it slow, waltz, don't boogie.

Or someone may share that their time is more important than money. Demonstrate that you will provide a high ROT—Return On Time. The opposite also applies. Then you need to illustrate how much money you will save them now or in the longer term.

Finally, some people are agree-ers and others are disagree-ers. Certain people naturally want to concur with you and others want to challenge you. If someone is an agree-er, it's easy. You move forward smoothly together. On the other hand, if someone is a disagree-er, you need to expect their resistance. You may even need to express a point of view that is opposite to where you want to go. For example, if someone tells me I'm too expensive, I tell them that they may be right. That motivates them to disagree with me and we get to a win-win.

It all comes down to the art of listening, which we'll explore next.

6. Listen like you mean it

One of the greatest gifts we can give anyone is the gift of intense listening. The age of disruption is also the age of distraction. Our attention spans can be measured in fifteen-second increments. People don't check out occasionally, they check in occasionally. Most of the time, they're preoccupied by sights and sounds that only they can see and hear.

Smartphones are the new cigarettes. It used to be that people would light up a cigarette to distract themselves. Now they consult their phones. We're hardwired to check our phones every time we hear the signal or feel the vibration. Even when we're not receiving anything, we check our screens in case anything has happened on

Facebook or LinkedIn over the past few seconds. We are making screen contact, not eye contact. We're looking down, not up. It's hard work making eye contact.

Think about how you feel when someone checks their phone while you're talking to them. Think about how the conversation is fatally interrupted. All it takes is for someone to check their phone even once and the connection with others is severed. The worst phrase you can use when you're in front of someone is "Sorry, I have to take this call." In that moment, you've reduced the other person to second-tier status in your life. No matter who you are, if someone else does that to you, it always hurts just a bit. People are segmented into two categories—those who pay full attention to you and those who check their phones while they're with you. Which one are you?

As Stephen Covey stated, "Seek first to understand, then to be understood." You can only communicate like magic if you understand what constitutes magic in the other person's mind. That means asking what I call the "Five Magic Questions":

- What do you think?
- How does that make you feel?
- Why do you think that is?
- What would you do?
- How can I help you?

If all you do is ask these questions in every conversation and then truly listen to the responses, you'll become someone other people choose to spend more time with. I'm amazed by the lack of questions in many marquee meetings. Either people are afraid to ask questions or they simply aren't interested in the responses. It takes genuine curiosity and confidence to ask the challenging questions. It also opens others up. It enables them to share insights that they otherwise would have kept hidden.

The best listeners listen

for what is not being said.

Then they surface the issue.

Disruptors bring up the

issues that others ignore

or gloss over.

Listen with your whole body, not just your ears. Physically immerse yourself in the conversation. We can sense things that are not being said when we're all in. We get "goosebumps" on our skin before we understand why we're so moved. We feel something in our stomach before we figure it out in our brain. We feel a tingle throughout our body that transcends reason. Literally, lean into conversations. Firstly, you'll hear a lot more. Secondly, you'll send out the signal that you're totally invested in the point of view of others. You'll notice immediate reciprocation.

Practice the smile of appreciation when you're listening to others. It's easy to smile when something is entertaining. But I'm talking about appreciation, not just amusement. If you show others that you enjoy being with them, almost all other sins are forgiven. Look around you in the next meeting. Watch how few people are visibly manifesting their delight in the presence of others. Then look at the most successful people and you will see that they are.

One of the most powerful phrases in the art of listening is, "What I'm not hearing is…" The best listeners listen for what is not being said. Then they surface the issue. Disruptors bring up the issues that others ignore or gloss over. As Sir Arthur Conan Doyle wrote in his legendary Sherlock Holmes story, "Silver Blaze," the fact that a dog did not bark during the night when a racehorse was removed from a stable was an important clue in solving the mystery of who had removed that horse. It was obviously someone whom the dog knew. How many incidents are there in your life where "the dog didn't bark"? Ask the question, because other people also want to know the answer—even if they weren't aware of it at the time.

Prove that you have truly listened to others by repeating their words to them, but seasoned with your insights. Begin with "So what I'm hearing you say is… " and then complete the thought. If you got it right, you'll have assured them that you're in sync. If not, you offer others an opportunity to correct you.

And when others say something to you that is astute or aligned with your thinking, state the magic word that will endear you to them, "Exactly!" People purr with pleasure when they're strongly reaffirmed by others. They want their voice to be heard. They want to matter.

However, before you can feed back what someone has said to you, you have to listen in the first place. So switch off the other voices in your mind when someone else is speaking to you. Dial up your fascination with their message. Actually use the words, "That's fascinating, tell me more." It's a discipline that grows stronger over time. The best time to begin is right now.

7. Focus your audience on their prize—it's all about the story

You and I share many things in common: we're both focused on becoming the kind of people that are extremely valuable to others. We both want to be disruptors, not disruptees. We both have a huge appetite for learning. We're both on a never-ending adventure. We're both committed to staying forever young. We both believe in miracles that we create together with others. We both want the public kudos that comes with being recognized for our contributions.

I've just focused you on the prize that motivated you to get this far. I've reminded you of the things that you value most highly. I've heightened your desire for the reward that makes all the training worthwhile, because that's the ultimate goal of everything I've shared with you so far. I'm focusing you on your desired outcome. I'm magnifying your dream in your mind. I'm cutting through what doesn't count so we can concentrate on what does. If we keep our eyes on the prize, the prize will pull us toward it.

People will go through disruption if they can see the promised land on the other side. The greater the disruption, the greater the promise needs to be. It's all about the story.

Stories are accounts of things that are fictional or real. They are narratives that inspire us to feel something or do something. They enrich our perspective. They influence our attitudes. They can even change our reality. The best stories clarify our course of action. They enable us to do things we could not have imagined before. That's why great books, theatre or news of true heroics make us cry. We experience through others what we would love to do ourselves.

We all have our favourite historical and fictional heroes. Mine are Nelson Mandela, Malala Yousafzai, Steve Jobs, Forrest Gump, Oprah Winfrey, Beyoncé, Anthony Bourdain, Stephen King, Braveheart, Jackie Robinson, Denzel Washington, Jerry Seinfeld, Malcolm Gladwell, Rick Grimes (from *The Walking Dead*), Winston Churchill, Bill Belichick and Richard Attenborough. Each one of them has inspired me to become who I am today and will be in the future. They're all larger than life. They represent the qualities that I want to stand for. I want to hear what they have to say, because their stories equip me to tell mine.

Great stories have three key ingredients:
- They have a plot—a sequence of events that build on each other in a satisfying manner.
- They captivate listeners so that they are transported into the world of the story.
- They have a theme that imprints itself in listeners forever.

Here's a mission for you, should you choose to accept it: tell me your story. Share your tale in a way that contains the above three ingredients. I guarantee that you will surprise yourself. You will clarify your own life themes. You may even experience your own breakthroughs.

Throughout this book, I have shared stories with you. Each one was designed to engage and educate you, in that order.

8. Make it as simple as possible, but no simpler

"I'm gonna make him an offer he can't refuse."
Michael Corleone in *The Godfather*

"Get busy living or get busy dying."
Andy Dufresne in *The Shawshank Redemption*

"Action expresses priorities."
Mahatma Gandhi

"Show me the money."
Jerry Maguire in *Jerry Maguire*

These phrases are simple but meaningful because they communicate a complex message in an instantly understandable way. Simple equals friendly, accessible, safe, comfortable, easy, energizing and actionable. When something occurs to us as simple, we don't question whether it can be done. We know it can be done. We won't second-guess ourselves. If it's meaningful enough, we'll take immediate action. Whenever we think, "I get it," we are imbued with an understanding that boosts our confidence and self-belief. You always want to be the person who makes people feel smarter and better about themselves. It's not about being the smartest person in the room. It's about making other people feel like they are the smartest people in the room.

> **You always want to be the person who makes people feel smarter and better about themselves.**

The three tests for simplicity are:

- How accurately can others replay your communication immediately after you've communicated with them?
- How much do they identify with your message?
- How clear are they on what they need to do as a result of your message?

Clever people appreciate simplicity. Ordinary people need it. Simple is elegant. Simple means that you've done the hard work so other people don't need to. But there is a line between simplicity and oversimplicity. In a flash, you can go from artist to charlatan. As-simple-as-possible requires integrity and intelligence in equal measure. Oversimplicity could be just plain stupid and myopic.

9. Use silence to speak

When I finish a speech and wait for the first question, there is always an uncomfortable silence until someone raises their hand. People look around to see if someone will ask a question. The seconds tick by. People become a little anxious. But I'm good with this kind of silence. I know people are thinking. I trust that someone will respond. And they always do—even if the pause goes on for longer than expected. People respond because I demonstrate my sense of ease with silence.

There are four kinds of silence:

- **Reflective silence**—When there's a lag between the invitation to respond and the actual response, it's a reflective silence. It's the space that people need to process what they've just heard. When we give people time to think, we show our empathy and our expectation that they will respond. However, you have to build your nerve to ensure that the quiet moments happen.

- **Receptive silence**—When other people are talking, your silence communicates your receptivity to their message. This kind of silence requires physical stillness and genuine eye contact. You show that nothing else is as important as the other person's message.

- **Dramatic silence**—Your main points need to be dramatized in order for them to stick. You can't take it for granted that people are even listening. Great communicators pause before they reveal their main point. They build suspense. They instill a sense of expectation. They also preface their message with a phrase that frames the message. For example, Steve Jobs would pause and say, "But we do have one more thing." I say, "What I'm about to share with you could be huge" or "This could be the most important insight I can give you." Then I make sure it's a big point!

- **Discouraging silence**—Human beings crave feedback, especially from people who are important to them. When we don't receive it, we fill the void with speculation as to why it wasn't given. Life isn't a poker game. Unless you're negotiating with an opponent, share your thoughts. Always be the first one to ask a question or make a comment—the person leading the conversation will be deeply grateful.

10. Master the new media

If you're a disruptor, you need to amplify your impact through every media platform that is available to you. Never step away from a microphone or a video camera that could broadcast your message to the maximum number of people.

The common denominator among disruptors is their ability to reproduce their charisma and passion by all available means. They sustain their spontaneity on camera. They ramp up their intensity on conference calls. They compress their messages in their posts. They tweet and Instagram appropriate images and thoughts.

No matter who you are, you can exponentially increase your influence by mastering the new media. There is an abundance of coaches who can advise you in this regard. Use them. Your return on investment will be spectacular.

At least half of all my work is sourced from people who have seen my videos, read my posts or heard my podcasts. The core insight here is to imagine your audience directly in front of you as you communicate. Talk exactly the way that you would talk if your most valuable stakeholders were directly in front of you.

I'll warn you right now that watching yourself on video is the one of the most painful things you can do. Our flaws and flubs seem far more acute to us than to anyone else. However, just like you need a lifeguard if you're swimming in the ocean, watch yourself with a trusted advisor who will give you perspective and guidance on how to enhance your impact. It never gets easier, but you will get better.

> **The common denominator among disruptors is their ability to reproduce their charisma and passion by all available means.**

Final thought: Defy gravity

The language of the disruptor is about defying gravity. It's about neutralizing the drag of the past with the pull of the future. It's transcendent, miraculous, beautiful, gorgeous, colossal, legendary, magical, herculean. It's so compelling that others suspend their disbelief to explore the possibilities that disruptors create for them. Nothing less will move people out of their safe place.

Some disruptors are natural orators. Others are inherently unfluent. However, when their desire for disruption is great enough, disruptors achieve extra verbal thrust. Either it comes from within or it comes from communication coaches like myself. Either way, every disruptor discovers how to combat the g-forces acting in the opposite direction to their acceleration.

I've used the language of lift-off throughout this entire book. From the first word to the last, I'm fixated on firing up your mojo. I'm using imagery and metaphors engineered to transport you into the stratosphere. And I'm having fun doing it. Can you tell?

If I were to listen to you, would I be motivated to leave home? Would I be willing to follow you into the void? Would I feel the rush of excitement that sweeps me along? Think about where you can amp up your communication octane to launch others into their self-actualization zones.

6

COLLABORATE
LIKE A
CHAMPION

From Aristotle to Zuckerberg, disruptors

transform their partners into powerhouses

they could never have become on their own.

They transform the process to enable others

to achieve unprecedented results. Their

mantra is "revolution through collaboration."

They are building an ecosystem of partners

that shares its genius. They attract the best

talent because the best talent goes

where it earns the highest return.

N SEPTEMBER 2014, Tony Bennett, aged eighty-nine, and Lady Gaga, thirty-one, launched their collaborative album, Cheek to Cheek. It was an audacious mash-up of artists from two completely different eras. Cheek to Cheek consists of jazz classics by such greats as George Gershwin, Cole Porter, Jerome Kern and Irving Berlin. It was an immediate hit. Debuting at number one on the Billboard 200, it sold 131,000 albums in its first week. Bennett also set the record as the oldest man to achieve a number-one album on the charts. So what's age got to do with it? Everything and nothing. At almost ninety years of age, Bennett drew on his legendary experience. Lady Gaga helped him make everything old new again.

By collaborating, Lady Gaga helped Tony Bennett disrupt the music industry by achieving the impossible—attracting young fans to his music, while still staying true to his roots as a classic crooner. It may sound counterintuitive, but if you are a great disruptor, you are also a great collaborator. Individually, Bennett and Lady Gaga are maestros of sound. Together, they are a once-in-a-generation phenomenon.

Anything I can do, we can do better: Loners are losers

There is no such thing as a self-made man. You will reach your goals only with the help of others.

GEORGE SHINN

One person may ideate the possibility, but it takes a community to bring it to life and then make it sing. Loners are losers. It's as simple as that. No matter how gifted one may be, one is an incomplete number. It can only go so far before it burns up or burns out. There is nothing more common than a disruptive person who cannot play nicely with others. It's cute in kindergarten, but it's self-defeating in adulthood.

The irony is that many of the most talented people in the workplace are also the least collaborative. In my work with over six hundred companies across the United States and Canada, I've discovered that only half of the top 20 percent of high performers are champion collaborators. Rob Cross, Reb Rebele and Adam Grant wrote in the *Harvard Business Review*, "We typically see an overlap of only about 50% between the top collaborative contributors in an organization and those employees deemed to be the top performers. But we also find that roughly 20% of organizational 'stars' don't help; they hit their numbers (and earn kudos for it) but don't amplify the success of their colleagues." In addition, they wrote, "research we've done across more than 300 organizations shows that the distribution of collaborative work is often extremely lopsided. In most cases, 20% to 35% of value-added collaborations come from only 3% to 5% of employees."[1]

You may be asking yourself how one can be a top performer without being collaborative. The answer is this: you can, but only for a short period of time. Top performers can achieve excellent results by sheer tenacity, work ethic, charisma, force of personality or knowledge. They can sustain their results until the project becomes too complex or interdependent to continue to thrive on their own. They tend to implode from the pressure of "taking on the world" by themselves. They become angry at or frustrated by their peers. Their egocentricity robs them of empathy and perspective. And they hurtle downward until they catch themselves or course-correct. Often it takes a cataclysmic personal event to alert them to their shortcomings.

I know. I speak from experience. I was the quintessential overachiever in the first decade of my career. I rose through the ranks of the global advertising agencies, Grey Advertising and Ogilvy & Mather. I was an exceptional account manager. I practised the first five of the seven secrets of dancing with disruption. But I was also impatient with my peers, intolerant of errors and dismissive of ideas that ran counter to my own. I hungered for personal kudos and the paycheque that came with it.

Then I hit the wall. I failed to enroll my colleagues in my cause. I couldn't deal with the pushback. I didn't orchestrate my resources effectively. I didn't commit to making others successful. In short, I didn't build the loyalty or trust of the people I needed most. I became stressed, depressed and exhausted. I resigned. I took time out. I re-evaluated my values, my style and my role. I reinvented myself as a coach, entrepreneur and motivator. I've come a long way, but I'm just starting.

Becoming a talent magnet:
"By invitation only"

Today, I know that success is "by invitation only." Unless you're still living in a feudal state, you cannot force anyone to want to work with you. Other people's commitment to you must be earned through your contribution to their well-being. We are only as successful as our ability to make others successful. My business is literally the business of motivating people to invite me into their organizations and to their events. It might begin with a call from them to me. Or they might approach me at an event after my speech. Or I might have reached out to them. But it's always a choice to hire me versus multiple competitive options.

The number one reason why people hire me is their perception that I am "the total package." I will understand their business. I will celebrate their people. I will bring everything I have to the moment. I will make it fun and transformative in equal measure. My clients become my team the instant the first contact is made. I immediately evolve our connection into "we," not "you and me."

Environics/Lipkin's research indicates that there are five core criteria that measure our commercial worth, contained in these questions:

· Am I turning my team(s) into champions?
· Am I consistently making a demonstrable difference?
· Am I extremely valuable to the people who are extremely valuable to me?
· Am I being invited to play bigger parts in bigger productions?
· Do the best people choose to partner with me?

On a scale of 1-5 how do you rate yourself on these five questions? Are you a four or five out of five on all of them? How do

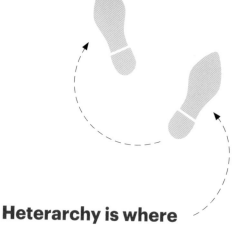

Heterarchy is where leaders and followers change depending on circumstances and clients. Heterarchy is defined by versatility, flexibility, adaptability, agility and personal discretion.

you know? Think about your response to each question. Write down your score and the reasons for it.

Anything south of four out of five makes you a "have-to-work-with" kind of person, not a "want-to-work-with" kind of person. The first kind makes work a grind. The second kind makes work a pleasure.

The more talented people are, the less they have to work with people with whom they have to work. The best talent goes where it will attract maximum appreciation. These people have earned the right to work with people with whom they want to work. The most talented teams also won't tolerate people who do not encourage that talent to become even better.

Hierarchy is so fifteen years ago. Today, heterarchy rules. Heterarchy is where leaders and followers change depending on circumstances and clients. Heterarchy is defined by versatility, flexibility, adaptability, agility and personal discretion. No client situation is ever the same, so there is no fixed way to handle any assignment. Collaboration is the only way to play. Unless people want to work with you, you'll be banished from the tribe. There are no badges of rank that give you automatic authority. There are only extraordinary results that inspire your peers to join your team or to invite you to join theirs.

You can tell immediately when you're in the company of want-to-work-with people. They radiate a chemistry that brings out the best in the best. It's a force field that magnifies others' capacity to be great. You feel yourself being challenged and rewarded in equal measure. You find yourself going further. You push yourself because you're being pulled forward by their passion.

Want-to-work-with people are always building reciprocity. They're always depositing into their goodwill accounts with others. They know that true wealth is measured in the number of people who are eager to repay them the favours that they've done for them.

After twenty-five years of researching and coaching high performers, I've discovered that people are programmed to return the favours they've received. The generous ones want to give back even more. It's better to give than to receive for one simple reason: you increase your currency of reciprocation. You build your reputation as a value-multiplier. You become a magnet for talent and opportunity.

Karla Congson is the poster want-to-work-with girl. She is a marketing powerhouse who held senior positions at global manufacturing and service companies before launching collective·iq, which is "an ecosystem of hand-picked expert free-agents, whose talent is harnessed to help our clients solve for their toughest business and marketing challenges." Karla and her partner, Natalie Serkin, describe their purpose and strategy as follows:

> We believe that... collaboration is the new competitive advantage. It's not just what you know that matters, rather, it's your ability to access the knowledge you need when you need it... Our tribe is made up of over 150 trusted independent freelance professionals, with whom we've had an average of five years in-the-trenches working experience. Our team includes brand strategists, cultural anthropologists, business analysts, writers, data scientists, creative directors, designers, marketing executives and more. In partnership with our clients, we help define the challenges they face and then we cast, curate and actively manage the right team of specialists to activate the optimal solution while ensuring the best cultural fit.[2]

Karla and Natalie specialize in being collaborative talent magnets. I've experienced first-hand their commitment to matching talent with opportunity. I have made it into the collective·iq tribe. It has won me multiple opportunities with blue-chip clients. We are joint mobilizers of opportunity for each other. I would do anything for Karla and Natalie because they have done so much for me.

So are you a want-to-work-with or have-to-work-with kind of person? When people know they will be working with you, are they overjoyed? Do they look forward to their meetings with delicious anticipation? Or are you a have-to-work-with kind of person who is just another reason why Monday is a downer?

Collaborative consumption and creation: The explosive rise of the sharing economy

Just a decade ago, it was inconceivable that you could share a stranger's apartment, car and driver, driveway and boardroom. Or that you could crowdsource logo-design services, corporate education, concierge facilities, investment advisors, fundraising and even insulin and pumps for diabetes. And that's just for starters. Consumers are choosing sharing over buying. It's part of the overall movement from owning things to experiencing things. It's about being free to choose not just the nature of the service or product, but the amount of time that you want to spend with it. Sub-par performance is instantly punished. Exceptional outcomes are rewarded with one more share.

The raging success of the sharing economy, where people are able to rent or borrow other people's assets, is having a major impact on the way many people work, live and play. Collaboration is being socialized and operationalized in every area of our lives. Its ubiquity is permeating our mindsets and influencing our perception of every service that we use—and especially our jobs.

The creature that best expresses the new collaborative reality is TaskRabbit. It's an online platform that enables you to "Get More Done in Less Time." It promises that its "same-day service platform instantly connects you with skilled Taskers to do your chores so you can be more productive, every day." TaskRabbit's mission is to "revolutionize everyday work."

Its value proposition is catching fire. According to Fast Company, "TaskRabbit has quadrupled annual revenue and is profitable in each of its 18 cities... TaskRabbit is now Ikea's exclusive service provider for help assembling items purchased at its London flagship."[3]

One of my biggest clients is a global bank with 4,500 people in sixty countries just in its accounting function. It has recently moved to a "shared services" model that has outsourced many of the "routine" services to an outside company. The one key factor that drove the decision was "the number of $100,000 salaries doing $40,000 jobs." The other key factor was the feedback from this accounting function's internal clients. They said that if they had a choice, they would hire someone else to perform their accounting function because they didn't believe they were receiving world-class quality. That was the wake-up call that my client needed. I'm happy to say that they now get top-box scores on almost every deliverable.

No matter what your role, your merit is being evaluated against its collaborative consumption and creation counterparts anywhere

The old mantra was "survival of the fittest." The new mantra is "revolution through collaboration."

in the world. The old mantra was "survival of the fittest." The new mantra is "revolution through collaboration." Either we're hunting breakthroughs together or we become the hunted. We need to leverage our invaluable face-to-face connection with the people we serve. We all bring something to the equation that no one else can: our unique personal touch. The questions are, how much value does your unique personal touch deliver? And how much is it valued by your stakeholders?

Collaborate: It rhymes with communicate, accelerate, cooperate and congratulate

Think about it: 80 percent of your time is spent in meetings, on the phone or responding to emails. Your engagement in collaborative activities has increased by 50 percent over the past five years. The complexity of your environment is accelerating even faster.

Some of your stakeholders will be on your direct team. Other stakeholders will be located elsewhere in your organization. Others will belong to partner companies, customers and suppliers. Still others will be part of networks that are still being formed. No matter who they are, you are in competition for their time, resources and belief in your ability to deliver a superior result. If you're not revolutionizing your workplace through collaboration, you're vulnerable to someone who will.

Ordinary collaboration is defined as working effectively with other people or groups to achieve a mutually desired result. Champion collaboration is defined as transforming the process to enable others to achieve unprecedented results. In the first case, you meet expectations. In the second, you redefine what's possible. You unlock the potential of the future. You expand the collective capacity of your community to be remarkable.

Amazon Prime: The power of one

I am consistently amazed at the power of one person to make a difference to an entire organization. Sometimes that person is at the top. And sometimes that person is on the front line, innovating while they serve their customers flawlessly.

The origination of Amazon Prime epitomizes this sentiment on all levels. A 2010 story in *Business Week* reported that after people join Prime, their purchases on the site increase by about 150 percent and may account for as much as 20 percent of Amazon's overall US sales.[4] The article tells the Amazon Prime story as follows:

> Prime came to life in late 2004, the result of a years-long search at Amazon for the right loyalty program. An Amazon software engineer named Charlie Ward first suggested the idea of a free shipping service via a suggestion box feature on Amazon's internal Web site. Bing Gordon, an Amazon board member and venture capitalist, says he came up with the "Prime" name, while other executives, including Chief Executive Jeff Bezos himself, devised the free two-day shipping offer, which exploited Amazon's ability to accelerate the handling of individual items in its distribution centers.
>
> According to several former employees who participated in the program's creation, Bezos commissioned Prime in December 2004 at an unusual Saturday meeting in the

boathouse behind his home in Medina, Wash. At the meeting, he told the small team of employees they could commandeer other company engineers and resources, and instructed them to ready Prime for a rollout in time for the company's fourth-quarter earnings report in January, less than two months away. The program is a "big idea," Bezos told the group that day in the boathouse, according to people who were there, and one that would help the company further capture the devotion of its best customers.[5]

This story has all the ingredients of champion collaboration: the sponsor at the top, the professional at the rock face, a culture of innovation and tolerance for failure, a massive commitment to customer satisfaction, an infrastructure for sharing, and a heightened sense of urgency. The rest is history.

You don't have to be Amazon to transform the process to enable unprecedented results. You can be a builder who cultivates a new way of customizing their offering to customers. You can be a salesperson who is committed to finding a better way and communicating it to their leadership. You can be a health care company that makes continuous dialogue with its "key opinion leader" physicians a cornerstone of their standard operating practice. You can be the entertainment company that makes contributions to teams outside its own the most important criteria for end-of-year bonuses and promotion. You can be the professional services firm that celebrates cross-discipline business-building that grows the entire suite of services. You can be the person who makes it a point to champion both your own ideas and those of others. But you have to make "revolution through collaboration" your personal mantra.

The smartest person in the room is the room

Joe Andrew, chairman of the global law firm Dentons, expressed his insights on being a collaboration champion in a June 2017 interview with the *New York Times*:

> The most important thing is having the humility to understand that it's about creating opportunities for other people. I love the phrase "The smartest person in the room is the room... The leader's job is to create the ability for people to feel comfortable to share their thoughts and ideas, whatever crazy thoughts they might have... Every single day, I go into a room of people that have succeeded since the day they graduated from kindergarten. They were the best in their class, they went to the very best schools, they do fantastically on standardized tests, the go to the best universities in the world, and they come out and make a lot of money. My job is to convince them that despite all those things, they've still got to change.[6]

You don't have to be the chairman to apply Andrew's wisdom. You just have to be someone who knows that champions are people who champion other people's points of view. If people are celebrated for sharing, they'll share a lot more.

In my sessions, one of the first things I promise people is that whatever they say, I will make them look good. I share that I'm only as good as the level of participation in the room. I thank my audience in advance for the invaluable contribution they are about to make. Then I make good on my promises. It's not difficult; it's enriching. There is no more rewarding sight for me than someone basking in the celebration of their point of view.

All families are expressions of collaboration. The healthier the family, the greater the level of collaboration. Everyone understands the role they play and its impact on other members of the family unit. The three roles of partner, parent and child are constantly shifting in response to the life cycle of the family and its circumstances. But they are always being played with other family members' well-being in mind. When this consideration breaks down, so does the rest of the family. Its functionality is directly proportional to the shared consciousness of the unit.

Coopetition is today's competitive norm

Did you know that "coopetition" is an actual word that appears in the Oxford Dictionary? It is defined as "collaboration between business competitors, in the hope of mutually beneficial business results."

At a macro-level, coopetition is a competitive norm. The challenges are too complex and too expensive for one company to solve, no matter how big it is. The biggest players form alliances with each other through partnerships and industry associations. When their collective success is on the line, I'm always amazed at how quickly people put aside their differences. As the old adage states, "The enemy of my enemy is my friend."

The real competitor isn't my competitor. It's ignorance, isolation and lost opportunities.

I'm called on to speak at many industry association meetings. Delegates go toe-to-toe with each other in the marketplace every day. Yet when the moment demands it, they also cooperate closely to champion their industry's interests. The same principle applies to our individual interests. Champion collaborators reach out to their competitors in the industry to share insights. They reach out to colleagues within their own organizations to do the same. They share notes where appropriate.

I have regular meetings with my most intense competitors. My intention is always to find out what my competitors know so I can use their information to grow my business. I know that's exactly their intention as well. But you know what? The real competitor isn't my competitor. It's ignorance, isolation and lost opportunities. I always take something valuable away from my conversations and I have never regretted sharing my knowledge. I share as much as I can without giving away proprietary information. That's why I'm writing this book. I know my competitors will read it. I've certainly read theirs.

The five barriers to collaborating like a champion, and how to convert them into springboards

So what gets in the way of champion collaboration? Why are there so few extra-milers? Environics/Lipkin's research has revealed five key barriers:

1. **Lack of purpose**—Collaboration requires a willingness to go above and beyond. It involves extra time and effort. People must believe it is worth it before they do it. Collaboration

happens on purpose, not by accident. If you want to be a talent magnet, you have to keep communicating compelling reasons why others should partner with you. Repetition makes you memorable.

2. **Lack of perspective**—Collaboration requires an understanding of the bigger picture beyond one's functional responsibilities. People must understand how their contribution impacts the greater whole. Disruptors have a peripheral vision that enables them to see the whole. They act as their stakeholders' eyes and ears so they can sense what's coming next.

3. **Lack of trust**—Collaboration is risky. It means putting your credibility in the hands of someone else. It requires a mutuality of interest where there is a reciprocal commitment to each other. Disruptors always follow through. They are their word. If they say it, they do it.

4. **Lack of expertise**—Collaboration is a dynamic discipline. It requires the agility, knowledge and technological savvy to shape-shift with one's environment on a daily basis. Disruptors are constantly upgrading their skills. They know that their personal edge goes blunt without continuous sharpening.

5. **Lack of enablers**—Collaboration takes off when there is a clear runway. It must be rewarded and systematized. It needs the culture and infrastructure to encourage its development. Disruptors build the hardware and the software to maximize collaboration. It's the discipline that sets them free to revolutionize their marketplaces.

Graham Rosenberg has converted all five barriers into springboards for success. He is the founder and CEO of Dentalcorp. This is a network of over two hundred dental practices across Canada with 3,500 staff members who provide dental care to over 10,000 Canadians a day. Here's how it describes its raison d'etre: "Our unique value proposition allows our Partners to retain their clinical and operating autonomy while we, as their business partner, provide comprehensive strategic expertise and tactical resources to support their growth. This enables our Partners to focus their energy on delivering optimal patient care."[7]

Dentalcorp's declared commitment is to "revolutionize the business of dentistry." It defines its mission as follows: "Our mission is to be a world-class business **Partner** for leading dentists across Canada. We **inspire** our Partners to achieve **ambitious** personal and professional growth. We provide unprecedented **strategic** insights and expertise that place our Partners at the **forefront** of oral care. We enable the best to be even better."[8]

Rosenberg and his team have achieved meteoric success by making collaboration a cornerstone of their constitution. Here's how Rosenberg defines it for his people: "We're creating a framework for exponential growth. We inspire each other to raise our game every day. We trust each other to support each other. Always. Every conversation builds our community and commitment to Great."

Context is decisive. When you operate within an environment that champions collaboration, you become a champion collaborator. However, at Dentalcorp, collaboration has a specific goal—to shake things up. Rosenberg promotes what he calls an "insurgency mindset." He says,

Insurgents are people who rebel against the establishment. They seek to topple the existing order. They see what's possible and they believe nothing is impossible. When others ask "why?" they ask "why not?" They play to win because losing is not an option. They are fast, lean, learning machines. They anticipate change and then make it happen. You can always recognize the insurgents—they are the ones shaking things up.

I have worked closely with Dentalcorp and its partners. They walk their talk. No matter what peoples' role within the organization, they're focused on redefining the way it should be played. That's why the company has been recognized as one of Canada's best places to work and an incubator of extraordinary talent. It is a gorgeous example of how to disrupt an industry by playing by the rules better than anyone else. By making collaboration a cornerstone of their constitution, Rosenberg and his team have achieved meteoric success. Dentalcorp has become so skilled at regulatory compliance that it has made it a competitive advantage to the benefit of its partners and their patients. When you don't have to worry about getting things wrong, you can focus all your energy on getting the right things right.

Disruptors don't necessarily "break the rules" (as the old cliché might suggest). Disruptors make the rules work for them because they understand them better than anyone else.

Forming, storming, norming, performing, adjourning

Psychologist Bruce Tuckman first came up with the memorable phrase, "forming, storming, norming, and performing" in 1965. He used it to describe the path that most teams follow on their way to high performance. Later, he added a fifth stage, "adjourning," which is also sometimes known as "mourning."

It's a framework that I have used extensively in my work with corporate teams around the world. As I walk you through the stages, ask yourself where your team is and how you as the leader or disruptor can take it to the next stage. In the age of disruption, your teams will be constantly changing and reconfiguring. You will find yourself going through the stages fast and furiously.

Forming

This is the start of the game, when the team comes together for the first time. In this stage, most team members are positive and polite. Some are anxious, as they haven't fully understood what work the team will do. Others are simply excited about the task ahead.

Storming

Next, the team moves into the storming phase, when members start to push against boundaries established in the forming stage. This is the stage where many teams fail.

Storming often starts when team members' work styles conflict. People may work in different ways for all sorts of reasons, but if they don't work in the same way as their colleagues, or if differing work styles cause unforeseen problems, people may become frustrated.

Storming can also happen in other situations. For example, team members may challenge each other's authority or jockey for position as their roles are clarified. Or, if the team hasn't clearly defined how it will work, team members may feel overwhelmed by their workload, or they could be uncomfortable with the approach that is being taken. Some may question the worth of the team's goal, and they may resist taking on tasks.

Team members who stick with the task may experience stress as they try to focus on the job at hand, particularly as they don't have the support of established processes or relationships with their colleagues.

Norming

Gradually, the team moves into the norming stage, when people start to resolve their differences, appreciate colleagues' strengths, and build a process for working with each other.

Now that the team members know each other better, they may socialize together, and they are able to ask each other for help and provide constructive feedback. People develop a stronger commitment to the team goal, and begin to see good progress toward it.

There is often a prolonged overlap between storming and norming, because, as new tasks come up, the team may lapse back into storming stage behaviour.

Performing

The team reaches the performing stage when hard work leads, without friction, to the achievement of the team's goal. This is supported by the structures and processes that one has set up.

Team members play at their full potential. They accelerate their personal development. The team's *esprit de corps* surges. Other people want to join in. It feels easy to be part of the team at this stage.

Adjourning

Many teams will reach this stage eventually. For example, project teams exist only for a fixed period, and even permanent teams may be disbanded through organizational restructuring.

Team members who like routine, or who have developed close working relationships with other team members, may find this stage difficult, particularly if their future now looks uncertain.

Using the framework

As a disruptor, your aim is to help your team reach and sustain high performance as quickly as possible. To do this, you will need to change your approach at each stage. Follow the steps below to ensure that you're doing the right thing at the right time.

1. Identify which stage of team development your team is at from the descriptions above.

2. Consider what you need to do to move toward the performing stage. Table 1 will help you understand your role and how you can move the team forward.
3. Schedule regular reviews of where your team is at, and adjust your behaviour and leadership approach appropriately.

Table 1: Forming, storming, norming, performing, adjourning

Step	Action
Forming	Direct the team, and establish objectives clearly. (A good way to do this is to create a team charter.)
Storming	Establish processes and structures, and build good relationships between team members. Resolve conflicts swiftly if they occur. Provide support, especially to those team members who are less secure. Remain positive and firm in the face of challenges to your leadership or the team's goal. Explain the "forming, storming, norming, and performing" idea, so that people understand why problems are occurring and see that things will get better in the future. Coach team members in assertiveness and conflict resolution skills where necessary. Use psychometric indicators such as Myers-Briggs to help people learn about different work styles and strengths.

Norming	Step back and help team members take responsibility for progress toward the goal. (This is a good time to arrange a team-building event.)
Performing	Delegate tasks and projects as much as you can. Once the team is achieving well, you should aim to have as light a touch as possible. You will now be able to start focusing on other goals and areas of work.
Adjourning	Take the time to celebrate the team's achievements. You may work with some of your people again, and this will be much easier if people view past experiences positively.

The twelve steps to being a champion collaborator

Let's bring it all together. The best time to become a champion collaborator is now. The best steps to take are the next twelve—one step at a time. If they work for you, pass them on.

1. Focus on what counts

Be clear from the start. Understand what you want to achieve through collaboration. Communicate it clearly. Help others define their compelling outcome. Know your primary goal and know why you want to achieve it. Know your personal strategy. Say no to the many things that don't count so that you can say yes to the few that do. Don't get sucked into distractions. Be clear on who you want to collaborate with—and who you don't. Own the outcome.

2. Give up things to get things

Let go of your preconceived personal agenda. Shift from "I want to get my way" to "I want to find the best way." Communicate your openness to others' opinions. Collaboration transcends negotiation. It's not me-versus-you. It's we're-only-as-good-as-all-of-us-together. Clear your mind so you make room for a whole new realm of breakthroughs.

3. Design a collaborative framework

Co-create the processes and structures that expedite success. Chart your course but be prepared to course-correct at any time. Build a culture that rewards collaboration and openness. Don't tolerate people who don't dance with others. Celebrate champion collaborators by telling their story wherever you can.

4. Build your stamina

Collaboration is intense work. You need stamina to go the extra mile. You need tenacity to hold on when others let go. You need resilience to turn setbacks into breakthroughs. The time to collaborate is when you're tired of collaborating. Keep the faith. Stay the course. It's the last nine yards that determine the success of the entire journey. As Vince Lombardi is reputed to have said, "Fatigue makes cowards of us all." Anyone can start strong. It's how you finish that counts. Talented people need "closers" to help them across the finish line.

Every company wants to be a great place to work, but how about the five to ten feet around you?

5. Promote your promise

Build your personal brand as a champion collaborator. Communicate your unique value proposition. Ensure that other people know how you can help them achieve their desired results. Use the language of possibility and opportunity. Never miss an opportunity to broadcast your benefit. We're all operating in a swirl of noise and confusion. Nothing about you is as clear to others as it is to yourself. Unless you declare your interdependence, others cannot know what you stand for. Say it. Do it. Repeat.

6. Use technology to amplify your impact

There's always an app for that. No matter what your industry, geniuses have created breakthrough tools to extend your reach and broaden your network. Choose your tools, then master them. Ask yourself, "How can I use this technology to create something with others that will be extraordinarily valuable in the marketplace?" Ask others for their opinion. The tools of collaboration are breathtaking. But first you need to decide to find them, use them and master them.

7. Create a collaborative presence

Every company wants to be a great place to work, but how about the five to ten feet around you? Is it easy for others to hang with you? Is your presence a great place to be? Do people feel invited? Or do they feel like they're trespassing when they come near you? Collaboration is a marathon. Make people want to run with you over the long haul. Express your confidence in them. Invite them into your ecosystem. Ask them how you can help them. Then follow through.

8. Be courageous

Becoming a champion collaborator means going where you haven't gone before. It means taking on new risks. It means that you go first so others can follow. It means making the best kind of mistakes. Fortune favours the brave. If you want to win, there is no other way to be. It's okay to be scared, just don't let it stop you.

9. Go looking for trouble

The view is always better when you're moving forward. There's always a breakdown waiting to happen. There's always a competitor circling your customers. There's always a gap about to open up. Find it. Talk about it. Partner with others to pre-empt it. Life is not an algorithm. Disruption is never routine. Nothing happens on command. You've got to earn others' followership over and over again. Prod people to do things they would never have done. They won't always be comfortable with you, but they'll always appreciate you later on.

10. Protect yourself against cynicism

Cynicism can become an excuse for not collaborating. Things go wrong. People are going to let you down. Your trust may be abused. Your motives may be misunderstood. Keep searching for new ways to collaborate. Keep giving more than you receive. Keep connecting great people to great people. No matter what happens, retain your belief in others. In the long term, the best people always come through for you. As the song by Journey goes, "Don't stop believin', hold on to the feelin'."

11. Get a cheering section

In South Africa, an imbongi is a praise-singer who precedes a chief by poetically proclaiming how great and wise the chief is. We all need an imbongi. We are judged by the calibre of people who sing our praises. Anyone can achieve anything if they have enough people championing them to succeed. So build your army of advocates. Give them reasons to mobilize others on your behalf.

12. Build the strength of weak ties: Develop a far-flung network

It's one thing to build your inner core. It's another thing to build your own personal World Wide Web that catches anyone, anywhere, who can champion your cause. This is when you need to leverage the strength of your "weak ties." Your inner circle isn't going to expand your network. It's your contacts who move in different circles that build your social eminence. Spend at least 10 percent of your time expanding the outer reaches of your network.

Final thought: The world champions of collaboration—Bill and Melinda Gates

How do you motivate the world's richest man to donate $24 billion to your charity? That's the amount that Warren Buffet has donated to the Bill & Melinda Gates Foundation so far. Buffet also committed the bulk of his estate to the foundation, which means there is a lot more to come. It helps that Bill Gates and Warren Buffet are best friends. But the real reason for the gift is the foundation's remarkable impact on the world's most important issues.

In their 2017 annual letter,[9] Bill and Melinda Gates express their mission in the following statements:

- Saving children's lives is the goal that launched our global work.
- We partnered with business and government to set up Gavi, the Vaccine Alliance, with the goal of getting vaccines to every child in the world. Gavi connects companies who develop vaccines with wealthy governments that help with funding and developing countries that get the vaccines to their people. Since 2000, Gavi has helped immunize 580 million children around the world.
- A big part of our work in global health is including the excluded—going to the margins of society and trying to bring everybody back in. For us, "All lives have equal value" is not just a principle; it's a strategy. You can create all kinds of new tools, but if you're not moving toward equality, you're not really changing the world. You're just rearranging it.
- Optimism is a huge asset. We can always use more of it. But optimism isn't a belief that things will automatically get better; it's a conviction that we can make things better.
- We've been using [Buffet's donations] to build an ecosystem of partners that shares its genius to improve lives and end disease.

Wow! When your goals are this colossal, the universe sends you Warren Buffet. This excerpt epitomizes the spirit and substance of champion collaboration: building "an ecosystem of partners that shares its genius." No one can it express it better than that. Can you imagine the kind of conversations that are required to pursue that kind of prize? Can you imagine the kind of people it requires? Can you imagine yourself being a part of it? How are you building your ecosystem?

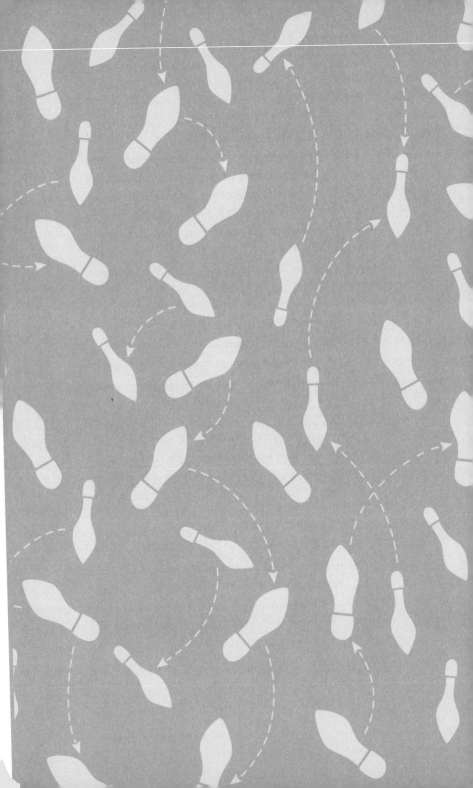

7

BE
UNCONDITIONALLY
ENTHUSIASTIC

Crises are how our lives are rerouted in
a new direction. Reversals will always
precede fast-forwards. If you're trying
to change the game, you've got to love the
game—especially when you're losing.
Enthusiasm doesn't mean exuberance.
It means being the best version of
yourself. Personal alchemy is the
transformation that occurs when you are
unconditionally enthusiastic. Follow
the code. Do it anyway.

REMEMBER THE SANDCASTLES you built as a child? Remember the sandcastles your child built? How long did they last? Did you worry about them collapsing or being washed away? No, it didn't matter. What mattered was building them and knowing that they would be swept away almost immediately. You didn't care about their longevity. You loved creating them. When they crumbled, you simply built another one. You were happy just doing it.

I am in the business of building sandcastles. I deliver keynote speeches for a living. I get up in front of people around the world and talk for sixty to ninety minutes. Then it's done. No matter how amazing my talk was, when it's over, it's over. The next speaker steps up or the audience breaks for lunch, coffee or dinner. I build my sandcastle in the air and then it's swept away. But the memories, the insights and the inspiration can last forever.

I am who I am because of the people who built sandcastles in my mind. They had an impact on me that became part of me. Their examples enabled me to excel. It wasn't the results that they were committed to achieving that impacted me, it was how they acted in the moment of contact with me. I remember their passion, their kindness, their wisdom and their generosity.

A "sandcastle mindset" is one that commits to creating the best product, solution or service in the moment, with whatever resources one has, with total engagement, without fearing the next wave. Everything has a half-life that is waiting to be replaced by the next version. The most we can do is the most we can do. If we do it, we can rest assured that we'll get to build another sandcastle directly after the next wave.

Disruption is an invitation to be the person you are most proud of

Most unforgettable moments happen during a crisis. That's when our lives are disrupted. That's when we have to reinvent ourselves. That's when we need to evolve to the next level. That's also when we experience the most pain. We lose things. We lose people. We even lose ourselves. Our success is directly proportionate to the pain we can bear. Happiness is the result of enduring misery, bewilderment, disappointment or bereavement. And yet that's when we have to be unconditionally enthusiastic about our lives.

Crises are the means by which our lives are rerouted in a new direction. They may occur to us as a disaster or a catastrophe at the time. They may seem unfair or even cruel. But if we become cynical or pessimistic in those moments, we give up the ability to turn them around. We also suck others down the rabbit hole with us.

As a disruptor, the deck will always be stacked against you. Reversals will always precede fast-forwards. That's exactly when you need to double down on your commitment to unconditional enthusiasm. The time to move forward is when things are going backward. The most important time to play like a winner is when you're losing or even when the game is lost. As Nelson Mandela said, "Do not judge me by my successes, judge me by how many times I fell down and got back up again." Or, as Churchill said, "Success consists of going from failure to failure without loss of enthusiasm."

The worst question you can ask yourself in times of crisis and disruption is, "What's the point?" If you want to lead, it's up to you to put the point into pointless. You define your circumstances, not the other way around. If you're reading this, you are not content just to go with the flow. You're not content to do nothing when you could do something. You want to be known as someone who can be counted on to make things better, especially when they seem to be getting worse.

We're only as good as the people we attract to us. Great people are attracted to great people. They vote with their legs—either they walk toward us or they walk away from us. No one walks toward people who disappear in the dark. Light and fire are integral parts of our job description if we want to change the game. We need to burn bright, but we can never burn out.

"You obviously love what you do"

When someone says to me, "You obviously love what you do," I know I'm already more than halfway to building a great relationship. On the other hand, if someone asks me, "Are you okay?" or says, "You look tired," I know I need to dial up my self-awareness. What do people think when they look at you?

When all else fails, you cannot. If you're trying to change the game, you've got to love the game—especially when you're losing. The title of this secret is "be unconditionally enthusiastic," not "be conditionally enthusiastic." It is a way of being that transcends your current situation. Apathy, lethargy, disinterest, pessimism, resignation and disheartedness are emotional states that disruptors cannot afford to indulge in. The first six secrets will give you the power to dance with disruption, but unconditional enthusiasm pulls the switch.

Enthusiasm is the agent of genius. It enables you to reach the levels that other emotions cannot get you to. It's not about being a Pollyanna who cannot see the downside. It's being someone who sees all sides and chooses to be fully engaged in achieving the desired outcome. Enthusiasm becomes your default position or you simply choose to play another game. Whatever game you play, you play full-out. Just going through the motions will get you nowhere.

See what's going on around you

Blinkers on horses are plastic eye cups that limit the animal's field of vision. By limiting what lies directly behind and around them, blinkers keep a horse from panicking. You're not a horse. Blinkers don't stop you from freaking out—they make you freak out. Panic and anxiety is heightened when we put restrictions on what we can hear or see around us. Desperation comes from a lack of options. Tunnel vision is terrifying if we don't like what we see.

Unconditional enthusiasm expands our aperture. It maximizes both the breadth and depth of our vision. It enables us to zoom in and to zoom out. It injects us with the endorphins and adrenalin to go deeper, further, broader. It's a sense-magnifier and circumstance-converter. When you have unconditional enthusiasm, anything is possible at any time.

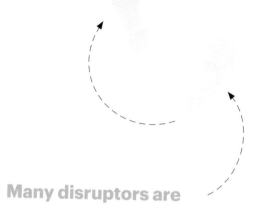

Many disruptors are

introverts by nature.

Research shows that introverts

account for up to half the

population. That percentage

increases the higher up

you go in the organization.

Enthusiasm doesn't mean exuberance—it means being the best version of yourself

The root meaning of the word "enthusiasm" comes from Greek for "having god within" (combining roots en, "in," and theos, "god"). When you're "éntheos," you're inspired by a higher power. You become the best version of yourself. You model the behaviour that you want others to demonstrate.

Enthusiasm isn't exuberance. You don't have to bounce off the walls to show off your passion. If you're naturally an introvert, then your enthusiasm will primarily be an inside job. It will be quiet and understated. This can be the most powerful kind of enthusiasm, because it's real and relatable. It doesn't intimidate or overawe others. It enables them to respond in a measured fashion. The question that you need to ask yourself is, "How can I naturally express my enthusiasm so other people are moved by it?"

Many disruptors are introverts by nature. Research shows that introverts account for up to half the population. That percentage increases the higher up you go in the organization. It may seem counterintuitive, but introverts make the best leaders. They listen more than they talk. They are calm and cool under pressure. They pass the kudos to their peers. They are planners and thinkers. In fact, behind most extroverts, you'll find an introvert pulling the strings.

One of the people who exemplifies the dance with disruption is Dani Reiss. Reiss is the CEO of Canada Goose, manufacturer of the eponymous and iconic parka. He is also someone who I brand as a "gifted introvert." By his own admission, he never intended to be a CEO, but I've watched him grow his business exponentially. He's a like a chess grand master, always planning three moves ahead. He is also unconditionally enthusiastic about his business and being an ambassador for Canada. Here's how Dani told me he manifests his unconditional enthusiasm for his coats, Canada and the cold:

> We are proud to be an ambassador for Canada as we export the Canadian brand around the world.
>
> Scaling our Made in Canada manufacturing has been a key focus and one of our biggest challenges. We decided early on that we wanted to keep making our core products in Canada, but then we were making 15,000 jackets a year. Now we make many, many hundreds of thousands each year. We have taken a leadership position in re-building a manufacturing infrastructure that didn't exist in this country at that time. It was the right decision then and continues to be today.
>
> I often tell people that we are the Land Rover of clothing. Land Rover is a functional product, built to endure extreme conditions, and it has become a luxury brand, but it wasn't built to be fashionable or a status symbol. We have collaborated with fashion houses and our jackets are sold in fashion retailers, but we've always been a function-first brand.
>
> Our jackets are often the first time people have truly felt warm during the winter. I've seen it happen hundreds of times. People put on one of our jackets for the first time and it's a life-changing experience. Suddenly, they start to look forward to bad weather.

Dani Reiss's unconditional enthusiasm overrides his introversion. At the time of writing, he was in Japan engaging in interviews with Japanese media. When you're on a mission, you're literally prepared to go to the ends of the earth to champion your cause.

By contrast, extroverts find it easier to reach out and touch people. They may be more adept at expressing their joy and excitement. They turn up the volume so everyone can hear. But they also have to be careful not to come across as slick and insincere.

Full disclosure: I am a pronounced extrovert in the workplace. I like being vocal. I like to wear my heart on my sleeve. I want people to see my joy at being around them. I laugh loudly and often. I'm the first to speak up or ask questions. I work very hard at being that way because it's my role. But I also have to be careful to avoid being branded as a loudmouth or an egotist. I moderate my behaviour based on my role and the audience I'm with.

In my personal life, I'm an introvert. I like to listen to my family and friends. I prefer being a spectator to being in the limelight. I find relaxation and comfort in letting others lead. My family even calls me by a different name because I am so different. At home, my name is Larrry—yes, with three r's. I am the butt of gentle jokes, not really taken seriously except when it's really serious.

At home, I project an image that is different from my professional persona because I'm playing a different role. It's an acute effort to be unconditionally enthusiastic at work, even though it is my default position. It never gets easier, but I'm becoming better at it. And you know what? All the extroverts I know work equally hard at displaying their enthusiasm. It doesn't come naturally to anyone, especially in adversity. The next time you see someone being an extrovert toward you, just know they're making an effort on your behalf. Reciprocate their response.

Tapping into one's divine spirit isn't a function of being introvert or extrovert. It's a willingness to explore the highest part of ourselves. It's a commitment to self-actualization. It's a hunger for fulfillment. It's a recognition of other people's need for acknowledgement. It's also an understanding that enthusiasm can be communicated in the subtlest of ways—a slight smile, a thumbs-up, a firm handshake, a gentle pat on the shoulder, a soft congratulation, a cheerful wink. In fact, the more introverted you are, the more impact even the smallest gesture has on the people around you.

Measuring your enthusiasm right now

Keep this test close. Take it all the time.

On a scale of 1 to 10 (1 being low and 10 being high), what is your level of enthusiasm at this moment?

8–10: The force is with you. You are in the zone. You're firing on all cylinders. You're clear, crisp and compelling. You feel like anything is possible. Your passion is propelling you forward. You're dancing with disruption and others are lining up to dance with you. Multiple opportunities are waiting to happen around you. You're pure potential in motion.

5–7: You're enthusiastic but you're not spontaneous. Your intentionality is driving you forward but it isn't automatic. You feel like you have to manufacture your enthusiasm in the face of setbacks or problems. You know what you have to do but it's hard to do what you know. The fire within is just a glimmer.

1–4: You're experiencing the opposite of enthusiasm. It could be disenchantment, boredom, ennui, discontent, unease, disappointment, fatigue, anxiety or frustration. You feel like you're on a treadmill going backward. Your thoughts are not flowing and your speech seems halting. You feel like you're faltering. It's only your tenacity and toughness that's pulling you through.

Where are you right now?

If you scored 8–10, mobilize your momentum. Fuel your fire. Seize every chance to strengthen your hand and play it to perfection. This is your moment to enhance every moment that follows. Make more calls. Have another meeting. Write a ground-breaking paper. Submit a proposal. Initiate another idea. Call a friend, or a colleague, or a client.

If you scored 5–7, savour the effort of trying to be unconditionally enthusiastic. Consciously build your enthusiasm muscles. Play your role. Practise being the way you would like other people to see you being. Step into your enthusiastic persona. Act "as if" you were an 8–10. Congratulate yourself for rising above your mood. Pay someone a compliment. Do someone a favour. Make a donation. Reach out to a close confidante for inspiration. Go for a walk. Eat a banana or apple. Listen to your favourite music. Tell your partner how much you love, adore and admire them.

If you scored 1–4, you need to step back or out of your everyday routine. You need to pull it apart so you can put it all together. Isolate the reasons for your malaise. Write them down. Evaluate them against the reasons why you love your work. Balance your downside with your upside. Get perspective. Talk to the people who really know. Call in your favours. Get professional advice. Do the work that needs to be done. Take a hard look at yourself and the competition vying for your business. Identify your decisive actions.

A miracle is just something that others don't believe can be achieved yet.

Take them. And celebrate your small victories as you climb out of the hole and into the warm light of unconditional enthusiasm.

The personal alchemy of unconditional enthusiasm: Follow the right code

The medieval forerunner of modern chemistry was alchemy. Alchemy is an ancient practice based on the supposed transformation of matter—in particular, ways to convert base metals into gold or to find a universal elixir. Alchemy is still alive and well and being practised by disruptors everywhere. They are the ones creating something out of nothing. They are making the impossible possible. They are translating ideas into things. They use bits, blocks and bytes to make people's dreams real even before people know it was their dream. Once they do it, it becomes obvious to everyone else.

Before you can transform anything, you first have to transform yourself. Personal alchemy is the transformation that occurs when you are unconditionally enthusiastic. If you follow the right code, you can create miracles. After all, a miracle is just something that others don't believe can be achieved yet.

"Code" is defined as a set of instructions for achieving a specific result; a set of standards governing one's behaviour in defined situations; a program where symbols are assigned specific meanings; a series of numbers that unlocks the answer.

Lipkin's Code for Unconditional Enthusiasm is a sequence of ten actions that will enable you to plug into your personal best at any moment. It guarantees that you will be ready for opportunity whenever it presents itself. It has been formulated through my research with Environics and my personal conversations with thousands of disruptors around the world.

1. Never forget why you joined: The thrill can never be gone

Tom Carroll is the VP Northwest, Las Vegas and Pacific Regions, at Tiffany & Co. At a session that I delivered to the Tiffany & Co. global leadership team in May 2016, I asked him what he regarded as the most important message I could share with his colleagues. Without hesitation, Tom said, "Never forget why you joined—to help people celebrate." Tiffany & Co. is in the business of celebration. It's a place that makes marquee moments memorable. Every person at Tiffany & Co. is an ambassador of celebration. They are expected to apply the "Tiffany Touch" to every guest. They cannot succeed unless they are genuinely inspired to help people celebrate.

Why did you sign up for your current mission? Can you remember? Can you communicate your motivation? Is it still a thrill? Are you living it? Can people sense it in you? I joined the business of motivation because I love inspiring hundreds of people at a time to do things they otherwise would never have done. Every year, it becomes even more thrilling because I know it's one year less that I get to do it. One hour on the stage is worth a month of preparing to get there.

If you can't remember why you joined, make up a reason now. If you can't make up a reason, find something that fires you up, because if you aren't fired with enthusiasm, you'll be fired with enthusiasm.

2. Declare your public persona: Who do you want others to think you are?

We are all three people: the person we think we are, the person we really are and the person we want others to think we are.

Life is a never-ending exploration in search of who we really are. Many of us may never uncover that truth. At best, we can minimize the gap between who we think we are and who we really are. But right here, right now, we can define who we want other people to think we are. Then we can act out that persona.

Declaration: Mike Lipkin's public persona

"I am 'the championator.' I help people become champions. I give them the inspiration and insights to play at their personal best. I am their go-to guy for breakthroughs. I enable miraculous outcomes."

I think I am the person that I want other people to think I am. It's taken me half a century to align those two personas. I endeavour to live my declaration every day. I'm using this book as a platform to share it with you because I want you to hold me accountable to it.

It's much easier to be unconditionally enthusiastic if there is alignment between who you think you are and who you want others to think you are. Then you need to train them to think of you that way.

In my seminars, most of the people in the audience do not know me personally. They form an impression of me based on my behaviour on stage. I ask for their opinions. Invariably, they brand me as someone similar to my declaration. So don't wait for people to judge you on your actions. Tell them what to expect and then make good on your promises.

Write down the declaration of your public persona. Does it excite you? Will it excite others? Have some fun with it. Share it. Refine it. Live it.

3. Develop your discernment: Be fascinated by what you find

Firefighters are fascinated by fire. They are detectives of "the burn." They understand the myriad kinds of fires, what causes them and how to extinguish them. Their lives depend on knowing what the fire is going to do next and how they must respond. Civilians stare at the same spectacle and see something very different. When it comes to fire, firefighters have a highly advanced level of discernment.

Discernment is defined as the ability to detect things that are not readily obvious to the untrained eye. It comes from asking questions that laypeople don't ask. It means looking for things that the uninitiated are not even aware of. It's cumulative—every day, more insights are gathered that enable you to build finer distinctions.

I'm a detective of inspiration. I'm fascinated by what uplifts people to achieve remarkable results. I'm passionate about probing the principles of high performance. I search for clues that can tip the scale in my clients' favour. I study coaches, teachers, entrepreneurs and leaders who empower their constituents to thrive on massive change. I love stories of triumph over trauma. I'm a collector of aphorisms and mantras that capture winning in a phrase.

I'm doing the work that needs to be done. Even though I love it, it demands total immersion. Every discovery makes me curious to find the next one. I record my lessons learned so I can make sure I've really learned them. As Stephen King said, "I write to understand what I think."

What are you a detective of? What fascinates you enough to keep you foraging for the next breakthrough?

> A mood is literally a temporary state of mind that induces specific emotions.

4. Master your moods: Sing the blues, don't get the blues

Singing the blues helps manage the blues. It's built deep into the genealogy of the genre. As jazz historian Ed Copp writes, "While blues lyrics often deal with personal adversity, the music itself goes far beyond self-pity. The blues is also about overcoming hard luck, saying what you feel, ridding yourself of frustration, letting your hair down and simply having fun. The best blues is visceral, cathartic, and starkly emotional. From unbridled joy to deep sadness, no form of music communicates more genuine emotion."[1]

Life isn't always sunshine and rainbows. No matter how charmed your life, there are going to be storms, earthquakes and tsunamis to endure. Your immediate emotional reaction may be dismay, disappointment, disturbance or even despair. That's natural and normal. Mere mortals can succumb to those emotions. They can crumble, fumble and cry over spilt opportunities or overturned dreams. They can blame others, curse their lives, go into a funk and sulk away into the sunset.

Disruptors, on the other hand, suck it up. They have built-in emotional shock absorbers. They take the hits. They feel the pain. They experience the loss. Then they sing the blues. They leverage their learning to lead their people. They accelerate their recovery time. They understand that pain is passing, but character lasts forever. They know that "this too shall pass quickly." They look beyond the breakdown to the breakthrough that is busy being born.

A mood is literally a temporary state of mind that induces specific emotions. In good times, our mood is automatically good. In bad times, our mood is automatically bad. But it's how we override our automatic tendencies that makes all the difference. Disruptors are not hijacked by their moods. They're conscious of the moods they're in. If the mood is negative, they find a way to make it positive. No matter what the external conditions, they find the sunshine within.

I am someone who needs to constantly override my automatic tendencies. I love to win. I love to share my insights with others. But when I lose an opportunity or encounter unexpected resistance, my natural inclination is to be angry, disappointed or frustrated—just like anyone else. That's when I need to take my own counsel and sing the blues. There is too much riding on the next call to dwell on defeat. So I will take a timeout. I'll go for a walk. I'll hug my dog. I'll treat myself to a latte or even something a little stronger. I'll call someone who is always happy to hear from me. I'll review positive feedback. I'll tell my wife how much I love her. I'll listen to B. B. King or Muddy Waters. Then I'll step back into the arena and pick up a phone...

Being a motivational speaker means never being able to say you're sorry. I can never apologize for a sub-par keynote if I'm being paid thousands of dollars to deliver it. There are too many people depending on the outcome, including me. My worst professional feeling is lamenting a poor performance. It's so painful that I make sure it never happens.

How do you sing the blues? How do you master your moods?

5. Be grateful to the game: To compete is glorious, to win is divine

If you're lucky, you become good at a game that you love. You win some, you lose some, but you always celebrate the competition.

Even when you lose, you're cognizant of the privilege of playing the game.

In 2014, I pitched myself as a keynote speaker at a global meeting of leaders from General Electric. I made it all the way to a face-off with one other speaker—a Harvard University professor. He won the gig. Even though I lost, I loved being in the same arena as one of the smartest people in the world.

I am often asked if I still get nervous before major events. The answer is a categorical yes, especially when I'm in a strange place and I wrestle with the demons of doubt in the dark of night. I call it the "rat hour," because that's when things gnaw at me. And the more worried I become, the less likely I am to sleep, which just ramps up the level of worry. I've discovered that sometimes there is no antidote to anxiety. You just have to go through it.

Are the sleepless nights worth it? Of course they are! When you are grateful to the game, you're willing to go through anything to compete. You endure the sleepless nights because you know they come with the territory. One of my CEO clients gets so nervous before presentations that he books himself into a hotel so his family doesn't have to endure his endless rehearsals and pacing. He hates the hours preceding his talk, but he loves the platform it gives him to share his message. Backing out is never a consideration.

I recently coached a woman who was afraid to speak in public, even though she knew it was necessary for her role in her company. As we prepared for her presentation, I asked her, "If your boss came by and told you that you didn't have to make the speech tomorrow, what would you say?" She answered, "I would be devastated." Her fear of speaking was dwarfed by her desire to play her role pre-eminently. She understood the merit of being anxious for the right reasons. I'm delighted to say that she delivered a spectacular performance.

"Standing tall" increases your

energy levels as it improves

the functions of your internal

organs and your lungs.

It also sends a message to

everyone around you:

I'm ready—bring it on.

Unconditional enthusiasm comes with conditions. You have to be willing to go through the agony to get to the ecstasy.

6. Stand tall, walk tall: Unconditional enthusiasm is physical

How do you think unconditional enthusiasm moves? How does it look? How does it sound? How does it feel? How does it even smell? Do you think it slouches, scowls or skulks? Does it look downcast or depressed? Does it sound ragged and resigned? Does it feel soft and soggy? Does it smell overripe or rotten? Obviously not.

Unconditional enthusiasm is robust. It is confident, bold, erect, grinning, fresh, resonant, vigorous, vital and vibrant. It feels like pride. It smells like action. It tastes like victory.

Try it now. Act like you're unconditionally enthusiastic.

I'll bet you sat up straight. You took a deep breath. You put a smile on your face. You radiated purpose. Stay like that. "Standing tall" increases your energy levels as it improves the functions of your internal organs and your lungs. It also sends a message to everyone around you: I'm ready—bring it on.

If you're still in doubt about what I'm saying here, watch the body language of opposing teams in any sport when the final whistle blows. The winners exhibit unconditional enthusiasm. The losers literally act like losers. Don't wait for the final whistle. Act like a winner every moment of every game.

When things go your way, it's easy to act like a winner. When they don't, you need to resist showing your discouragement. I make a point of reacting with zeal and zest when I hear bad news. I smile. I laugh. I exclaim, "Well, all good things must pass. Every story has a beginning, a middle and an end. I'm still on a never-ending roll. This is a bump in the road, not the end of the road. With all this crap, there must be a pony in here somewhere." Often

I surprise prospects with my bonhomie and good cheer. They respond with admiration and respect. Soon afterwards, they find another opportunity for me.

7. Widen your social circle: New people renew you

In December 2015, I travelled to Milan, Italy, for an assignment. As I entered the Milan airport, I was struck by how stylish people were. This impression was only enhanced when I arrived at my hotel, the Westin Palace. The doormen, the concierge, the taxi drivers, the bartenders, the shop attendants, even the panhandlers, displayed an effortless style that enchanted me. I had never been surrounded by such uniform elegance before.

When I remarked on the ubiquitous stylishness to my client, he told me it was a Milanese trait. He said there was even a word for it: *sprezzatura*. It means a "studied carelessness." It's a style that seems natural and spontaneous, but it's an integral part of the culture. He told me that it's taken the Milanese centuries of effort to make it look so easy.

Matteo Bologna is *sprezzatura* incarnate. Bologna is a Milan-born designer who has designed a range of reading glasses called Ottavo—that's Italian for "finally, reading glasses that don't suck." The glasses epitomize *sprezzatura*, blending colourful boldness with sensuous curves to create optical art. The mantra for the brand is "See in Italian." Bologna and his team express Ottavo's ethos as follows: "Say hello and goodbye in the same word. Take three hours to eat a meal. Argue with friends and kiss your enemies. Arrive late, stay later. Mix breaking news with bikinis. Bring wine to a protest. Read the menu by candlelight."

My Italian client changed my view of the world with a single word: *sprezzatura*. It's become my antidote to stress and strain. Just saying it makes me chuckle. I've tried to permeate this book with its spirit. It's also why I travel to Italy every year.

Some people collect stamps. Others collect watches, cars or paintings. I collect people. New people are the source of almost all my content. Every conversation is an introduction to a new concept that wasn't on my radar before. The more different the other person is from me, the greater my delight in adding them to my network. Acquiring new perspectives by talking to new people is one of my great pleasures.

But I'm talking about real live conversations, not digital fakes. I'm talking about getting F2F—face to face. We need to look into other peoples' eyes, listen to their points of view and visit their worlds. We need to get out of our familiarity zones. All the cheese is located where we've never been before. So become a traveller, both literally and figuratively. It doesn't matter whether you're an introvert or an extrovert—let your love of people sweep you along.

The person with the widest social circle wins. Broaden your milieu, broaden your horizons. Expand your success.

8. Be easily wowed: Every day, see the magic in the everyday

Dave O'Neil is the general manager of Zimmer Biomet Canada, a leading medical device and joint replacement company. He is a remarkable leader who has built a great business and one of the widest professional networks in his field. Besides his knowledge and experience, O'Neil's signature strength is his tendency to marvel at even the smallest events. He celebrates every positive thing that happens to him. He listens openly to every point and communicates his approval with gusto. Even when he disagrees with others, he lets them know that their point is still a fine one. Eating even a basic meal with him is rewarding. He leaves nothing on his plate. When something big occurs (like winning a major new account), or when someone achieves great results (like changing a patient's life with breakthrough technology), or when consuming excellent food and drink, O'Neil really exclaims his appreciation. His favourite phrase is, "That's shocking." He is always stunned to the upside, no matter how many times he goes through the experience.

Disruptors like O'Neil are childlike in their enthusiasm. They are amazed by their everyday realities. Nothing gets old for them. They see everything again for the very first time. It's more than just being aware of their good fortune. It's being enchanted by it. It's a lifelong party to which everyone is invited. This kind of enthusiasm is contagious. You cannot remain unmoved in its presence. You find yourself thinking, "O'Neil is right. It is shockingly good. I didn't think of it like that before."

"Wow." It's such a small word with such an outsize impact. It's the way we express spontaneous excitement or astonishment. It's also the way we impress or captivate others. It's synonymous with thrill and joy. Just saying "wow" gets you closer to feeling the "wow." I make a point of expressing my feeling of wow as often as I can. If I see or hear anything that is pleasing, I exclaim it with the conviction I authentically feel. I've discovered that people love the sensation of wowing others. If I give it to them, some of that sensation is simultaneously transferred to me.

Right now, I'm surrounded by wow. Literally everything I look at wows me: a wall of books, a Lamy fountain pen, Bose noise-cancelling headphones, hundred-year-old trees, a finely grained oak table, a Persian carpet, handmade furniture, and today's issue of the New York Times. Each item is a source of immense pleasure. There may be ugly in the world. But there's much more beautiful. Wow.

9. Take your eye off the scoreboard, focus on the game

I'm coaching Chris, a forty-five-year-old entrepreneur who sold his company to a Fortune 500 organization. It took him twenty years to make his business worth the $30 million they paid him for it. However, part of the purchase price was contingent on future earnings. Four months into the acquisition, he was 20 percent behind his first year's target, and $3 million was on the line. Chris became fixated on the shortfall. All he could think about was not meeting other people's expectations. Rationally, he understood that the initial deficit could be made up. Emotionally, he became obsessed with the deficit. He made it the centre-point of his communication with his team. Day after day, he harangued them about not making target. He emphasized the downside and elucidated the threats. The revenue continued to decline.

That's when I started working with Chris. I pointed out that the shortfall was a direct consequence of the previous year's focus on doing the deal rather than running the company. I advised him that he was experiencing the delayed effect of his diverted attention. I assured him that if he concentrated fully on playing the game like a champion, the scoreboard would reflect the desired result. He got it. He easily blew past his target.

The scoreboard is a reflection of what has already occurred. Watching it won't change it. If you want to change it, play the game the way it's meant to be played. This spirit is epitomized in a description of the British and Irish Lions rugby team's draw with the New Zealand All Blacks in their third and final international game in July 2017 in Eden Park, New Zealand. Oliver Holt reported in the *Mail Online*:

They gave it everything. They played as if there really was no tomorrow. As the All Blacks pummelled them, somehow, through sheer bloody-mindedness, a refusal to give in and some uncharacteristically poor handling from the world champions, the Lions hung in there... There is another interpretation of this drawn series, too. It was proof of the unrelenting determination of both sets of players not to be beaten. They were so desperate to win that none celebrated at the end. But none were vanquished either and there is great nobility in that. Rugby is rarely for the faint-hearted and these Lions pushed themselves to their limits and sometimes beyond... There is no Sunday for these Lions. There is no day after. There was nothing more they could have given.[2]

If you can say that about you and your team, the scoreboard will ultimately show you what you want to see. Life is tough but so are you. You will always prevail, eventually.

10. Train like an athlete

With every stride, the brain has to answer four questions: are you going to stop, go the same speed, speed up, or slow down?
DR. TIM NOAKES, **professor of sports science, University of Cape Town, South Africa**

No athlete makes it to the Olympic Games without a training program that prepares them for it. Natural gifts merely give you permission to play. Here is a brief description of Michael Phelps's training routine, as reported in *Muscle Prodigy*:

In peak training phases, Phelps swims a minimum of 80,000 meters a week, which is nearly 50 miles. He practices twice a day, sometimes more if he's training at altitude. Phelps trains for around five to six hours a day at six days a week... Phelps does long swims to improve his endurance. However, he does other drills to improve his swimming speed and form. He does a lot of vertical kicking and underwater kicking... Phelps recently added a weightlifting regimen to his dry-land

> **Health and well-being are variables we can control: 80 percent of longevity is lifestyle, not genes.**

work... He lifts weights 3 days a week, preferably on Monday, Wednesday and Friday. However, Phelps prefers bodyweight exercises like pushups and weighted pull-ups for muscular strength and endurance. [He] keeps a great balance between bodyweight exercises and weight exercises.[3]

Unconditional enthusiasm takes Olympian stamina. We literally need to be fit to lead and inspire others. Health and well-being are variables we can control: 80 percent of longevity is lifestyle, not genes. And the older we get, the more important our lifestyle becomes.

Disruptors can sustain their level of intensity because of their investment in their mental and physical fitness. The best investment you can make is an investment in your personal vitality and well-being. If you want to age well, train like an athlete. It's the best immunization against degeneration and dementia.

All the disruptors with whom I'm working, irrespective of age, are zealous about their well-being regimen. Their gym is their fourth place after their work, home and Starbucks. They are conscious consumers of their food and drink. They schedule the time to decompress through leisure, meditation or philanthropy. They go on courses. They set themselves inspiring goals. For example, when my wife and I take our annual trips to Greece and Italy, we set ourselves a goal of walking twenty-five kilometres a day. It's a fabulous way to build our stamina while we get up close and personal with our destination.

When your brain asks, "Are you going to stop, go the same speed, speed up, or slow down?" what are you going to answer?

Final thought: Do it anyway

Kent Keith is a Harvard-educated writer and teacher who wrote *The Paradoxical Commandments* in 1968. Half a century later, his commandments are even more powerful than they were then. They also encapsulate the ethos of unconditional enthusiasm:

People are illogical, unreasonable, and self-centered.
Love them anyway.

If you do good, people will accuse you of selfish ulterior motives.
Do good anyway.

If you are successful, you will win false friends and true enemies.
Succeed anyway.

The good you do today will be forgotten tomorrow.
Do good anyway.

Honesty and frankness make you vulnerable.
Be honest and frank anyway.

The biggest men and women with the biggest ideas can be shot down by the smallest men and women with the smallest minds.
Think big anyway.

People favor underdogs but follow only top dogs.
Fight for a few underdogs anyway.

What you spend years building may be destroyed overnight.
Build anyway.

People really need help but may attack you if you do help them.
Help people anyway.

Give the world the best you have and you'll get kicked in the teeth.
Give the world the best you have anyway.[4]

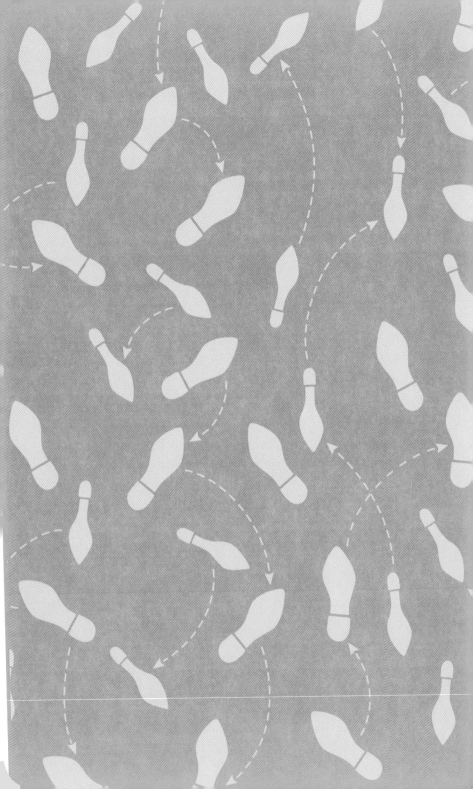

MY FINAL CALL TO ACTION: PUSH THE ENVELOPE

T'S THE NIGHT of the 2020 All-Star Disruptor Awards for my clients and readers. They are being recognized for their revolutionary contributions to their communities over the past two years. Five thousand business and thought leaders are gathered in a grand auditorium. Millions more are watching on television and online. A hush falls as the envelope is opened. When the name is announced, everyone jumps to their feet in a standing ovation. I recognize the name as one of my most loyal clients. I'm wowed beyond measure. The noise finally subsides and as the winner begins to speak, I hear the words I dream about every day:

"First of all, I want to thank my family, my team and my closest associates for helping me become an all-star disruptor. I especially want to thank my coach, Mike Lipkin, for giving me the inspiration and insights that made all the difference."

The next award is announced and once again the winner thanks me for my contribution. So does the next and the next. Over the subsequent twelve months, another million people around the world earn their All-Star Disruptor Awards because of my inspiration and insights. This is the audacious dream that gets me out of bed every morning. This is my amazing chase. This is my constant search on your behalf.

Disruption is not a one-time event. It's a discipline that needs to become part of your DNA. It means seeing every day as day one. It's the opposite of cruising to the finish line. It's not for sissies or those who are afraid of angst. It requires a humongous appetite for learning. It demands the kind of character that cares deeply, even too deeply, about pushing the envelope.

Pushing the envelope means exceeding the limits of what is normally done. It has nothing to do with paper and correspondence. It is an aviation term that refers to the technical limits of a plane's performance. It refers to pilots testing their skill at the very edge of a plane's capacity for speed and stress.

Disruptors know that they have to dance at the very edge of their capacity. No matter how gifted they are, their aspirations are always going to stretch them. That's how they know they're giving it their all. They just can't give any more. Their domain doesn't matter. You can be a barrista or a barrister, a mechanic or a mathematician, an artist or an actuary, but you've got to want to reinvent the way your work is done.

It's a constant connection to an essential drive. As Theo Epstein, the president of baseball operations of the Chicago Cubs, said, "When people do things they weren't even sure they were capable of, I think it comes back to connection. Connection with teammates. Connection with organization. Feeling like they belong in the environment. I think it's a human need—the need to feel connected. We don't live in isolation. Most people don't like working in isolation—some do, but they typically don't end up playing Major League Baseball."[1]

I hope this book has connected you to the thing that makes you magical. I hope you're inspired to do the things that you'll regret not doing. My wish for you is that your epitaph will read, "She did all she could with all she had. She played all the music she had within her. She danced until she ran out of breath."

So what kind of disruptor are you going to be? What are you going to commit to doing to make the dream real? What's your personal envelope? I'm committed to helping world-class talent win their own All-Star Disruptor Awards. I want to be the one they thank when they broadcast their thanks to the world. This book is a deposit on my commitment to being the best coach to people who have entrusted their development to me. What's yours?

Speaking of All-Star Disruptor Awards, Kevin Spacey epitomizes the endless quest for innovation through his performance in *Clarence Darrow*, the acclaimed solo show about the legendary lawyer, written by David. W. Rintels and directed by Thea Sharrock. First presented at the Old Vic in London, Spacey brought the show to America for a unique two-night event at Arthur Ashe Stadium in Flushing, New York, in June 2017.

Mr. Spacey first came across the play when he was in high school. The one-man show made its Broadway debut at the Helen Hayes Theater in 1974. The real Clarence Darrow was a courageous man at the turn of the last century. He was a lawyer who steadfastly accepted cases nobody else would take, fighting on behalf of the underdog and standing up for labour unions as well as being a staunch opponent of the death penalty during a career that spanned over forty years. Through his dignity, intelligence and logic he often managed to convince judges and jurors to change their view, shift their prejudice and opt for a humane punishment on behalf of those he defended. Spacey brings Darrow to life over the course of ninety minutes, in which Darrow with his legendary wit relives some of his extraordinary experiences and the infamous trials that established his reputation as a courtroom giant and civil rights hero.

Announcing the production, Spacey said, "Clarence Darrow was one of the most important attorneys in the United States and I just love the idea of Darrow and Arthur Ashe coming together:

I want to "remind" you to keep

dancing through the disruption,

the danger and the confusion.

"Remind" is the most important

word in my vocabulary.

It means I keep the seven secrets

front and centre in my mind.

both masters of two very different courts. Of course, drama happens all the time on Ashe, but never quite like this. I love a new challenge and this is an exciting opportunity to share Darrow's remarkable story with a broader and more diverse audience than usually gets a chance to see theater."[2]

Variety magazine raved about Spacey's performance:

> Actually, one never gets the feeling one is watching Clarence Darrow—it's all Kevin Spacey, showboating for a wide variety of New Yorkers and their out-of-town friends (and 350 students, to whom the Kevin Spacey Foundation donated seats) by bringing them to a kind of theatrical political rally. Every time Spacey speaks of winning a case for a vulnerable client, the audience cheers, and after a while you get the sense that this venue, with its awful sound, pungent smells, and flip-up seats, is exactly where this event is meant to happen. Like Trump's rallies, it is theater for the American people, only this time we know that the great man is good.[3]

I have shared stories of giants throughout this book because we all need to stand on their shoulders. Their achievements are famous. That's why I've quoted them. They're recognizable. But your achievements are far more valuable to the people who matter to you. They are the ones that count. They are also counting on you. You are one of those people to me.

We've come a long way together. But this part of the dance is almost over and the next one is about to begin. I want to "remind" you to keep dancing through the disruption, the danger and the confusion. "Remind" is the most important word in my vocabulary. It means I keep the seven secrets front and centre in my mind.

If, every day, I am the one who really knows, if I have an audacious dream, if I am simultaneously analytical and creative, if I am prolific, if I communicate like magic, if I collaborate like a champion, if I summon my unconditional enthusiasm, I know I will win by becoming the person who helps others win. I write to remind myself to be who I need to be. Also, if I declare my intention publicly, I have to walk the talk. There's no going back on my words.

There is something powerful in getting the words out of your head and onto the page. It enables you to see them out loud. It also enables you to share them. Others can see exactly what you've written. They can provide their perspective and their support. They can help you make sense of things that didn't make sense before. It takes multiple partners to help you dance with disruption, and first they have to know exactly what you want to do.

Eventually, we all become the company we keep. If you want to see where you're going, look at the people with whom you spend the most time. Hell is spending most of your time with people you don't like, trust or admire. That's the route to personal eruption. Disruption calls for people who've got your back because they want to pull you forward.

The main thing is to keep the main thing the main thing. The minutiae can bury us. The urgent issues can sweep us away. We can die by a thousand cuts every day. We all need people who can lift us up. Without guides, we can get lost. I've played the role of your co-pilot here. Every point in the book is a coordinate on your journey to success. Now you need to play that role for others.

There's no time to waste. Whatever happens, hunt breakthroughs and expect miracles. You'll be surprised at how often you'll achieve both. And that's a reason to dance, dance, dance.

ACKNOWLEDGEMENTS

I took a chance on Jesse Finkelstein and her team at Page Two Strategies. Jesse made big promises and she followed through big-time. Without her process, skills, encouragement and discipline, this book would never have got done.

I also want to thank my colleagues at Environics for providing me with the insights and environment to do great work. It's been seventeen years of great partnership.

Finally, I want to thank my wife, Hilary, for always being there to support and champion me through all the trials of publishing a new book.

NOTES

Introduction: You Have to Be a "Bit Mad"—Like Macron, Varadkar and Bezos

1. "Marchons, marchons!" *Economist* (May 13, 2017).

2. "Emmanuel Macron's Quest to Reform France," *Economist* (May 13, 2017).

3. David Streitfield, "Whole Foods Deal Shows Amazon's Prodigious Tolerance for Risk," *New York Times* (June 17, 2017).

4. Tim Blair, "Run, Hide, Repeat," *Daily Telegraph* (June 5, 2017).

5. Joseph Brean, "Terror Attacks Giving West a Sense of Daily Israeli Life, Jerusalem Mayor Says," *National Post* (June 7, 2017).

6. Leigh Gallagher, "The Original Hospitality Disrupter," *New York Times* (June 8, 2017).

7. "The Creed of Speed: Is the Pace of Business Really Getting Quicker?" *Economist* (December 5, 2015).

8. City of Toronto, "City of Toronto in Partnership with 100 Resilient Cities Appoints Elliott Cappell as Toronto's First Chief Resilience Officer" (press release, June 15, 2017). www.publicnow.com

9. Melissa Hogenboom, "The Traits That Make Human Beings Unique," BBC Future (July 6, 2015). http://www.bbc.com/future/story/20150706-the-small-list-of-things-that-make-humans-unique

1. Become the Person Who Really Knows

1. Phyllis Rose, "Into the Twentieth Century—Two Toronto Bridges," *Canadian Journal of Civil Engineering 11* (1984): 875–883.

2. "Genchi Genbutsu: More a Frame of Mind Than a Plan of Action," *Economist* (October 13, 2009).

3. Ibid.

4. Tim Harford, "What We Get Wrong about Technology," *Financial Times* (July 6, 2017).

5. Bill Taylor, "The Best Leaders Are Insatiable Learners," *Harvard Business Review* (September 5, 2014).

2. Be an Audacious Dreamer—Sell Your Unicorn to Pharaohs

1. Stephanie Petit, "Swimmer Ryan Murphy Wrote a Letter to His Parents at Eight Years Old Declaring His Olympic Goals; Now He's a Gold Medalist," *People* (August 9, 2016).

2. "Solar Roof" (May 10, 2017). www.tesla.com/en_CA/blog/solar-roof

3. Tom Randall, "No One Saw Tesla's Solar Roof Coming," *Bloomberg Technology* (October 31, 2016). www.bloomberg.com/news/articles/2016-10-31/no-one-saw-tesla-s-solar-roof-coming

4. Martha Stewart. *The Martha Rules: 10 Essentials for Achieving Success as You Start, Build, or Manage a Business* (New York: Rodale, 2005), xi.

5. Smriti Bhagat, Moira Burke, Carlos Diuk, Ismail Onur Filiz, and Sergey Edunov, "Three and a Half Degrees of Separation," Facebook Research (February 4, 2016). https://research.fb.com/three-and-a-half-degrees-of-separation/

3. Be Simultaneously Analytical and Creative

1. Mark Wilson, "Adidas's Secret Weapon in the Sneaker Wars," *CO.DESIGN* (April 17, 2017). www.fastcodesign.com/90110021/adidass-secret-weapon-in-the-sneaker-wars

2. Debra Kaye, "Four Tips to Master Thinking with Both Sides of the Brain, and Boost Creativity," *Fast Company* (August 15, 2013). www.fastcompany.com/3015721/4-tips-to-master-thinking-with-both-sides-of-your-brain-an

3. "Idea Generation: Divergent vs. Convergent Thinking," *Cleverism* (April 29, 2015). www.cleverism.com/idea-generation-divergent-vs-convergent-thinking

4. Debra Kaye, "Four Tips to Master Thinking with Both Sides of the Brain, and Boost Creativity," *Fast Company* (August 15, 2013). www.fastcompany.com/3015721/4-tips-to-master-thinking-with-both-sides-of-your-brain-an

5. Ian Brown, "Eyes Wide Open," *Globe and Mail* (March 30, 2017).

6. Ibid.

7. James Dyson, "Yes, It's OK It Took Me 5,127 Attempts to Make a Bagless Vacuum," *Globe and Mail* (August 11, 2014).

8. Rupal Parekh, "Global Study: 75% of People Think They're Not Living Up to Creative Potential," *AdvertisingAge* (April 23, 2012).

9. Environics Analytics, "London Fire Department with Partner Environics Analytics Wins Prestigious Canadian Marketing Award" (March 24, 2015). www.environicsanalytics.ca/footer/news/2015/03/24/london-fire-department-with-partner-environics-analytics-wins-prestigious-canadian-marketing-association-award

10. Eric R. Danton, "Beyoncé Surprises with New Album Release," *Rolling Stone* (December 13, 2013).

4. Be Prolific

1. Jamie Millar, "Wahlberg's Workout," *Men's Health* (UK) (October 10, 2016).

2. Lawrence Pearsall Jacks, *Education through Recreation* (1932).

3. "About James: Biography." www.jamespatterson.com/biography#.WawWMq0ZORt

4. Todd Purdum, "The Henry Ford of Books," *Vanity Fair* (January 2015).

5. Jonathan Mahler, "James Patterson Inc.," *New York Times Magazine* (January 20, 2010).

6. Gallup, State of the American Workplace (February 2017). www.gallup.com

7. Nitsuh Abebe, "America's New 'Anxiety' Disorder," *New York Times Magazine* (April 18, 2017).

8. Beth Comstock, "Who Likes to Fail?" *NewCo Shift* (May 30, 2017). https://shift.newco.co/who-likes-to-fail-3a4784f550ce

9. Mallory Schlossberg, "While the Rest of the Industry Struggles, This Store Has Created the 'Best Business Model in Apparel'—and Millennials Are Flocking to It," *Business Insider* (June 16, 2016).

10. Ibid.

11. Suzy Hansen, "How Zara Grew into the World's Largest Fashion Retailer," *New York Times Magazine* (November 9, 2012).

12. Brent Schrotenboer, "Bill Belichick Didn't Flinch in Super Bowl Comeback, and Patriots Followed His Lead," *USA Today* (February 6, 2017).

5. Communicate Like Magic

1. Herminia Ibarra, "The Authenticity Paradox," in *HBR's 10 Must Reads for New Managers* (Boston, MA: Harvard Business Publishing, 2017).

6. Collaborate Like a Champion

1. Rob Cross, Reb Rebele, and Adam Grant, " Collaborative Overload," *Harvard Business Review* (January/February 2016).

2. "Our Story," collective·iq. www.coiq.com/our-story/

3. "Why TaskRabbit Is One of the Most Innovative Companies of 2017," *Fast Company* (February 13, 2017).

4. Brad Tuttle, "How Amazon Gets You to Stop Shopping Anywhere Else," *TIME* (December 1, 2010).

5. Brad Stone, "What's in Amazon's Box? Instant Gratification," *Business Week* (November 24, 2010).

6. Adam Bryant, "Joe Andrew on Building a Culture to Encourage Creativity," *New York Times* (June 23, 2017).

7. "About." www.dentalcorp.ca/site/about

8. Ibid.

9. Bill Gates, "2017 Annual Letter," GatesNotes (February 14, 2017). www.gatesnotes.com/2017-Annual-Letter

7. Be Unconditionally Enthusiastic

1. Ed Kopp, "A Brief History of the Blues," All About Jazz (August 16, 2015). www.allaboutjazz.com/a-brief-history-of-the-blues-by-ed-kopp.php

2. Oliver Holt, "Lions Leave Nothing Behind as Warren Gattland's Men Do the Jersey Proud in Dramatic Draw Against New Zealand," *Mail* (July 8, 2017).

3. Richie Allen, "Michael Phelps Workout and Diet," *Muscle Prodigy* (December 11, 2011). www.muscleprodigy.com/michael-phelps-workout-and-diet/

4. Kent M. Keith, "The Paradoxical Commandments." www.paradoxical-commandments.com/index.html

My Final Call to Action: Push the Envelope

1. Tom Verducci, *The Cub's Way: The Zen of Building the Best Team in Baseball and Breaking the Curse* (New York: Crown Archetype, 2017), 50.

2. Jeremy Gerard, "Kevin Spacey Will Appear in (Tennis) Court as Clarence Darrow," *Deadline Hollywood* (April 26, 2017). http://deadline.com/2017/04/kevin-spacey-clarence-darrow-1202078161

3. Trish Deitch, "Theater Review: Kevin Spacey as 'Clarence Darrow' in a Tennis Stadium," *Variety* (June 16, 2017).

START A CONVERSATION WITH MIKE

Talk to Mike about how he can help you and your
team dance with disruption through his customized
live seminars and workshops.

ENVIRONICS/LIPKIN
RESEARCHED MOTIVATION & PERSUASION

33 Bloor Street East, Suite 1020
Toronto ON Canada M4W 3H1

416.969.2822

mike.lipkin@environics.ca
www.mikelipkin.com